ENJOYING HOME CARPENTRY AND WOODWORK

ENJOYING HOME CARPENTRY AND WOODWORK

F. E. Sherlock

with illustrations by
John Binks

WILLIAM LUSCOMBE

First published in Great Britain by
William Luscombe Publisher Ltd.,
The Mitchell Beazley Group,
Artists House,
14—15 Manette Street,
London, W1V 5LB
1976

Text set in 11 pt. Photon Imprint, printed by photolithography,
and bound in Great Britain at The Pitman Press, Bath

This book is dedicated to
the memory of my father,
the woodturner,
who enchanted me with his use of wood
when I was young
and fell in love easily

Acknowledgements

The making of any book is always an effort in co-operation; this one is no exception. My teaching colleagues have, without complaint, allowed me to question them continually on their own special ground in order to check and verify my detail.

My close colleague, Peter Saggers, for this, the second time round, read and checked the manuscript, and my friend Audrey Caplin typed through the winter months to produce the final work for the printer.

The following companies willingly sent me information that I requested:

Stanley Bridges Ltd.	Electric Power Tools
Myford Ltd.	Machine Tools
Izal Ltd.	Wood Finishes
Black and Decker Ltd.	Portable Electric Tools
Record Ridgeway Education-Service	Hand Woodworking Tools.

A special mention must be made of Charlie Jones, who, with his sons, runs one of the larger 'Home Handyman' supply centres, at Bullsmoor, in Enfield, North London.

Charlie has allowed me to browse through his stock, poking and prying, trying and testing. He himself probably knows how to use every item he sells; we were, at one time, both furniture men together.

To all of these I express my sincere thanks.

F. E. SHERLOCK

Contents

Preface

Out of the blue came the suggestion that there was a need for a book written to help boys learn about woodwork in their own homes. I felt that there were so many such books available that one more would be more than enough. So I looked.

I found to my surprise that there were in fact very few such books, and those that there were, were either 'How to Make' books, or were examination text books for G.C.E. Woodwork.

Out of this I planned this book. The scope was stretched to take in the interests of 'boys' of seventy as well as boys of seventeen. I have hoped, during writing, to interest people in wood, and in how to use it; to explain the 'whys' and 'wherefores' of each tool and of each method. If I have been successful then maybe I have opened the door of interest to those who *Would Work with Wood!* There is no better material with which to dabble from seventeen to seventy and beyond.

F. E. SHERLOCK

Glossary of Terms

The following list of words is intended for easy reference should a quick definition be required. It is not definitive and the entries have been worded in as simple a manner as possible. The text of the book itself contains reasonably comprehensive explanations of the technical terms used.

F. E. Sherlock

Adhesive	Alternative and more correct name for glue.
Ampere (Amp.)	The unit of measure of a flowing electric current. The flow rate.
Annular Rings	Rings formed when the yearly growth cycle of a tree stops.
Architrave	A moulding applied as a cover strip over the joint between a door frame and the wall.
Auger	A long twist bit for boring through joists.
Back Saw	Any saw having a back strip along its blade.
Bark	Protective cork covering of the growing tree.
Bevel	An angled edge to a section. The tool used for marking bevels.
Bit	A tool for boring used in a drill or brace.
Block Board	A sandwich of wood strips between thick veneers.
Brushes	Carbon contacts that conduct electricity from wires to the commutator of an electric tool.
Cap Iron	The shaped plate that holds a plane iron in place.
Carcase	Any box-like construction—a cabinet.
Carcasing (Timber)	Low grade softwood for construction work.
Carpentry	Timber components of the house. The act of making such components.
Chamfer	An edge only part bevelled.
Chipboard	Board made from glued and pressed wood chips.
Chuck	That part of the brace that grips the bit.
Cill (Sill)	The foot member of a door or window frame.
Commutator	The copper ring that picks up current from the brushes in an electric motor.
Cross-cutting	Cutting across the grain.
Dead Knots	Loose knots.
Deal	Trade name for yellow softwood.
D.P.C.	Damp Proof Course. Impervious film in wall base.
Double Insulation	A specific term meaning that both frame and the motor of an electric tool are fully insulated from earth, and from each other. No earth wire required.
Dovetail	A form of joint where dovetailed shape tails fit into like shaped sockets.

Dovetail (Box)	A form of dovetail where tails are visible on both outer faces of the joint.
Dovetail (Lap)	Where tails only 'lap' into the ends of the socket member.
Earth	The essential path to 'earth' should a wiring fault occur in an electric tool.
Emulsion	A two liquid mixture where one carries the other as a very fine dispersion.
Felling	The cutting down of the tree.
Ferrule	The brass ring surrounding the end of a tool handle to prevent splitting.
Filling	Grain fill by plaster-based material.
Finish	Surface finish. A coated protection to wood.
Fitting	Final adjustment of one part to another. Metal or plastic 'fittings'.
Fixing	Process of fixing wood frames and wood trim to house structure.
Folding Wedges	Two wedges that slide on each other to apply thrust.
Forming	Producing shaped ply by laminating veneers on shaped moulds.
Frog	Angled seat for plane iron. Centre recess in bricks.
Fuse	The protective 'weak link' in an electric circuit.
Glue	Liquid or semi-liquid adhesive.
Grain	General lie of wood fibres.
Head	The top cross-member of a door or window frame.
Heartwood	The darker, more solid centre of a board.
Hand Brace	A cranked tool for rotating boring bits.
Hand Saw	All saws that have no back strip and are not held in tension by a frame.
Hangers	Metal brackets from walls to carry joists. Vertical members from roof timber to ceilings.
Hardboard	Wood 'pulp' board.
Hardwood	Broad-leaf tree timber: Oak, Beech, Chestnut, etc.
Hip	The corner angle of a sloping roof.
Honing	The final sharpening of a tool.
Hot-melt	A quick setting adhesive that changes from solid to liquid and back within a narrow temperature range.
Housing	A grooved joint across width of material.
Insulation	A barrier to bar electricity, heat or sound.
Jack (Plane)	General purpose plane.
Jack (Rafter)	The rafter that is cut between wall-plate and hip rafter.
Jamb	The vertical side member of a door or window frame.

Joists	Floor and ceiling timbers to which the boarding is nailed.
Kerf	The width of a saw cut.
Kiln	The heat chamber in which timber is dried.
Knot	The embryo branch centre.
Knotting	A shellac mixture applied to seal exudation of resin from knots that are under a paint film.
Laminate	Thin veneer. One of a layered pack.
Laminated Board	Thin strips glued face to face and then sandwiched edge-on between thick veneers.
Level	Horizontal. The tool used to check levelness, which incorporates a bubble in a curved glass tube.
Low volt	Electric tools working on less than mains voltage. 110 v not 240 v.
Man-made Wood	Plywood, Chipboard, Blockboard.
Marking Out	Marking lines on wood to indicate cuts required.
Matt	A dull, non-gloss surface finish.
Moisture Content	The amount of moisture in wood expressed as a percentage of its dry weight.
Mortise	The slot that receives the tenon in a mortise and tenon joint.
Movement	Shrinking, twisting, bowing as wood dries.
Mullion	A vertical, intermediate frame member.
Muntin	An intermediate rail, carrying panels.
Noggings	Horizontal rough members of a timber partition.
P.A.R.	Planed all round.
Partition (Stud)	Wood wall faced with plaster board.
Pinch rods	Two long thin laths used to measure openings.
Plane	To make 'plane'—flat. The tool used for planing.
Plane Iron	The cutting tool of the plane. No longer 'iron' but carbon steel.
Ploughing	Groove cutting.
Plywood	Layers of veneer bonded to make a flat sheet.
Polishing	Surface finishing with a shellac-based material.
Pressing	Cramping. Mainly flat sheets—veneering.
Primer	First finishing coat to raw wood prior to painting.
Purlins	Roof timbers that run parallel to ridge across lower sides of spars or rafters to support them.
Rafters	Spars. Roof timbers angled from wall plate to support ridge, or apex.
Ridge	Roof timber horizontal along length at highest part. The apex supported by rafters.
Rip sawing	Sawing along the grain.

Riser	The rising board in front of a stair step.
Rod	Full size drawing. Sections through a proposed job. Used to make cutting list and for direct marking of wood prior to cutting.
Rubbed Joint	Square edged boards glued together without mechanical key.
Sanding	Smoothing with abrasive paper.
Sapwood	The lighter and less dense band of wood around a tree. Prone to insect attack and shrinkage.
Sash	A glazed frame. A window hinged, sliding or fixed that is fitted into the window frame.
Scarf	A lengthening joint usually tapered.
Scribing	Fitting one shape to another—skirting to floor, or moulding to moulding.
Seasoning	The controlled drying of wood.
Section	A 'cut through'. An end view.
Setting	Applying set—side clearance to saw teeth. The curing or drying of glue.
Shakes	Splits in wood due to drying.
Shrinkage	Loss of size as moisture dries out.
Skirting	A board that 'skirts' a room at floor level.
Softwood	Needle-leaf tree timber.
Spars	Rafters. Roof timber angled to apex from the wall plate.
Staining	Dying or colouring wood to leave grain showing through.
Stile	Vertical side members of window sashes or doors.
Stopping	Hole filling prior to finishing.
String	Side member of stair flight.
Struts	Herring bone (diagonal) strutting between floor joists. Roof timbers from purlins to interior walls.
Studs	Vertical roughwood member of a 'stud' partition.
Summer Wood	Cells formed in spring. Large cells reducing as the year grows old.
Tang	The tapered and pointed handle end of the metal part of a chisel or file.
Taper Saw File	A triangular, tapered file for saw sharpening.
T. & G.	Tongued and grooved (flooring–boarding).
Templet	Template. A shaped pattern for marking.
Tenon	The tongue of a mortise and tenon joint.
Thermo Setting	Glue that sets only if heat is applied and is non-reversible.
Thixotropic	The property of a jellied glue or paint to thin out and slide under pressure and thereafter to set or re-jell as pressure is removed.

Thyristor	A solid-state electronic component that breaks an electric current into regular impulses. Basis of electric tool speed control.
Timber	The bulk material—wood. Applied to construction material.
Tongue	The piece that fits to the groove in a tongue and groove joint.
Transformer	Electric device to transform high voltage into low voltage for low-volt tools.
Tungsten Carbide	Materials used to make hard tool tips for such as masonry drills.
Tread	The level board trodden on in a stair flight.
Truss	A timber roof frame (triangulated) that sits on wall plates and supports ridge, purlins and rafters.
Volt	The unit of pressure of an electric current.
Veneer	Thin sheet (of wood) of superior nature to cover an inferior base.
Wall Plate	House timber along top of walls.
Watt	The unit of measure of power output of an electric device.
Wedge	A small tapered piece of wood used to apply pressure and to secure tight fitting of joints.
Wheel-brace	A mechanical brace that rotates small drills when a handwheel is turned.
Wood	The bulk material—timber. Applied when pieces are of small size, intended for use in specific jobs.

1 From the Tree to the Wood

Trees grow! We all know that. We all know, too, that trees, when they are cut up, give us wood; wood that we use for carpentry, cabinet making, carving and sometimes for burning.

What we don't all know is how the tree grows, how the manner of its growth affects the nature of the wood it produces and—more important to us—how the nature of the wood causes us trouble if it is awkward or coarse, or makes work easier if it is fine and mild.

TREE GROWTH

Trees grow by adding layer upon layer of cells to the outside, starting with the centre pith, which, enclosed with a thin skin of wood, is the sapling, or young tree. The cell layers increase because each previous layer divides.

Soil moisture is drawn up through the roots and through the tree cells by the suction created when the sun plays on the leaves and evaporates moisture from them. More moisture must come up to replace that which is lost to the air. This is called TRANSPIRATION, the process of circulating water through a plant and out to atmosphere, and back to the land in the form of rain.

The sap rises through the inner portion of the trunk and then travels outwards along the branches to the leaves. Here the chemical loaded moisture is changed to tree food by PHOTOSYNTHESIS, which is the act of changing the state of the tree-borne chemicals into plant food by the action of sun and air. The air provides OXYGEN and CARBON DIOXIDE.

The plant food created at the leaves moves back into the tree where it feeds and creates more cells by division. These cells are the small, tube-like cavities of which the tree is built. The shape, nature and size of these cells determines the quality and type of the wood that the tree will eventually produce.

The growing area is on the outside of the tree below the BARK, or protective coat covering that falls away from time to time as the tree grows. New bark then forms.

Inside the bark there is a soft lining called BAST which protects the next layer, the growing one, called CAMBIUM. The newly created tree food descends into the cambium layer where it creates the new cells as the old ones divide.

As the year warms up in the spring, the sap rises. It is called by the sun and begins to promote growth. This early summer growth is rapid and cells formed are large. As summer progresses, growth slows down and only smaller cells are formed. As summer ends, growth ceases, and we are left with a complete ANNULAR ring of cells around the outside of the tree. Thus each ring, when looked at with a good magnifier, has a porous appearance at its inner side and a much more solid appearance at its outer limit. This limit denotes the end of growth for one year.

In addition to this yearly cycle of growth a much more important change takes place in the tree. In order to stiffen the trunk and to give stability, the centre of the tree begins to LIGNIFY. This means that true wood is being formed. The inner mass of cell walls swell and become solid. No further growth takes place and the hardness and lack of tree food protect the centre area from the foraging grubs of the insects that attack wood. This darker area of tree centre is called HEARTWOOD and is the wood best suited for most uses.

Meanwhile, the outer bands of wood, averaging about a sixth of the tree, remain light coloured, not so hard, and full of sap. For this reason it is called SAPWOOD, and is to be discarded if the carpenter wants his work to last for a long time. Because of the starchy tree food found in the sap, any part of sapwood will attract insect borers and the spores of fungi. It is not always economically possible to discard all sapwood, but it is the ideal at which to aim.

DEFECTS OF SAPWOOD

Wood-boring beetles attack sapwood. They lay eggs in any rough surface they find during the summer. The egg becomes a very small grub, with very strong jaws. It burrows down into the wood, growing larger as it goes, and, of course, making a long hole or tunnel. This grub, or LARVAE may burrow for several years, travelling in the sapwood and living in the sap left in the tree when it was felled. Sooner or later the larvae goes into PUPATION, or chrysalis form, and after resting for a while in the cavity which it has previously bored for this purpose, emerges in the early summer as an adult beetle. It bores to the surface and flies away, leaving its flight hole as the only sign of passage. When the wood is cut, the many tunnels, filled with the dust of digested wood fibre, are exposed. The adult beetle flies on to deposit a further supply of eggs in its turn.

There are three main types of beetle, all having roughly the same activity. The largest is the DEATH WATCH BEETLE, which attacks old beams and rafters. Then there is the POWDER POST BEETLE whose presence is often only detected by the presence of fine dust on the floor under furniture. The smallest is the FURNITURE BEETLE which tends to attack furniture made with sapwood.

THE STRUCTURE OF WOOD

Wood from trees is made up of millions of small tube-like cells, each cell laying close to its neighbour. The cell walls are fibrous and are mainly made of CELLULOSE. The manner of the linking, and size and type of the cells, determines the final nature of the wood; whether it is to be mild and easy working, or tough, fibrous and difficult. Each type of tree has its own grain peculiarities.

When the tree is felled (cut down), there will be sap trapped in the sapwood. This will now start to dry out. Firstly the free water within the cells will migrate to the outside and evaporate. Then the cell walls will dry out. At this point trouble may start for the carpenter. The wood shrinks.

SHRINKAGE
As the cell walls dry out, so each cell shrinks. Layer upon layer, row upon row, the cells get smaller, and the wood loses weight, for water is heavy stuff. Remember now that the sapwood bands circle the tree and that the heartwood is firmly built in the centre. Unequal shrinkage will take place, for the sapwood has nearly all of the moisture to lose, whilst the heartwood has very little. The sapwood will shrink much more than the heartwood and distortion must take place, or the wood will split.

The round log will shrink inwards. The heart of the tree will resist. But shrink the sapwood must. But it cannot go in, so it splits. All around the outside splits will develop.

If the log has been cut into boards before drying begins, then each board will react to loss of moisture according to the part of the log from which it is cut. A board cut from the centre will not move (shrink) much at all, whereas a sapwood board will shrink very much. Even this is not the whole story for as the outer board of the log has more cells packed into it than any inner board, there are more cells here to shrink. Then any board will shrink more on the face that was nearest to the outside of the tree than on the inner face that was towards the tree centre. The board will curl up, and always curl away from the heart. If, in addition, the board has been cut before the log has lost much moisture, it will shrink according to the part of the tree from which it is cut. A board cut from the centre will not move (shrink) much at all, whereas a sapwood board will move very much. A further complication is possible, for it may well be that there are both sapwood and heartwood in a board. The resulting movement may make the board twist. Defects of movement are shown in Fig. 1.

A good carpenter will design his job and select his wood with shrinkage in mind, for even finished woodwork absorbs moisture in winter from the air and loses it again next summer. Movement will spoil good jobs, so allowance must be made for loose fitting of those parts that must move. Construction details will be dealt with later.

Fig. 1.
a A solid wood top will split if it is screwed down.
b Shrinkage plates will allow such a top to move and not split.
c Floor construction allows free air circulation to prevent fungi attack due to dampness under floor.

d Feather-edged boarding is fixed with one nail per board to allow movement. Skirting with 'heart-side' to the wall will curl away. Flooring laid with high moisture-content boards will shrink and curl.

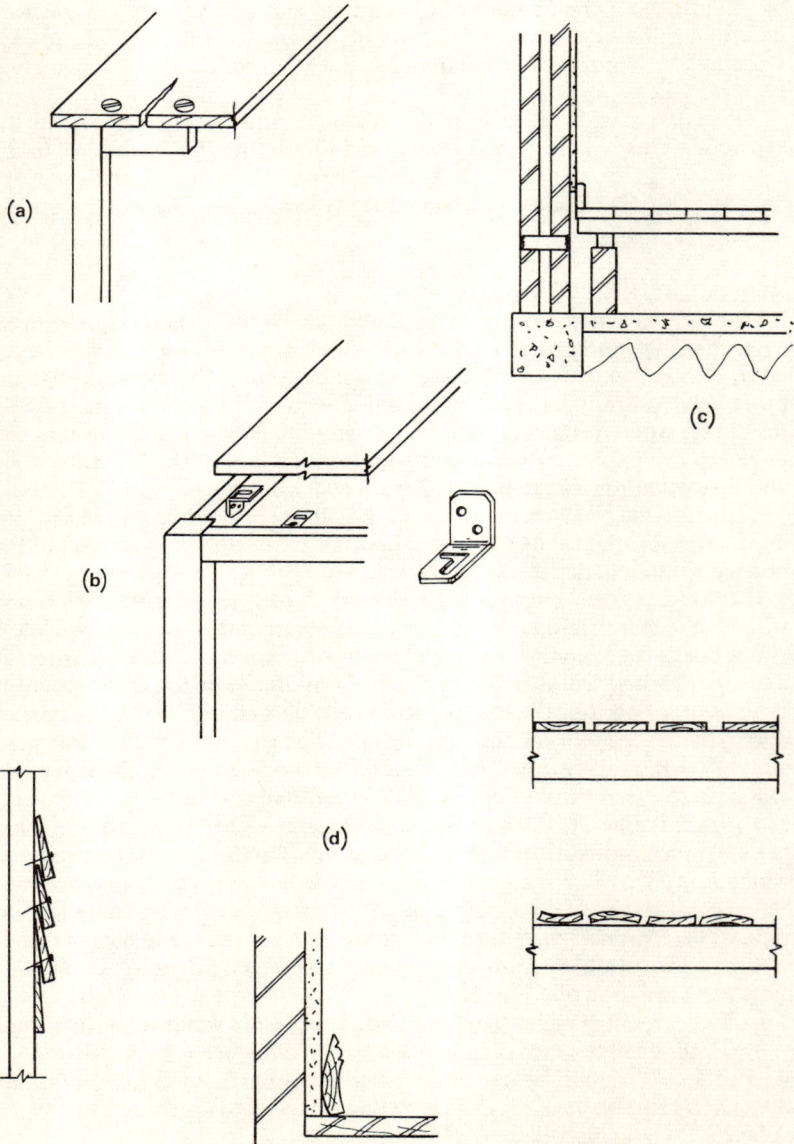

(a)

(c)

(b)

(d)

OTHER DEFECTS

Knots are branch centres. They are the 'M' way junctions where cell layers fight to travel their own way; where new shoots begin a new beginning and disruption occurs to GRAIN lines. Grain is the general lie of the wood cell layers. Knots are strong and solid and are reasonably easy to work. They are sometimes unsightly and are then cut away to waste. They may cause structural weakness in building wood, and their size and spacing is closely watched by the good carpenter.

Some knots are dead. They have died during the tree life and shrink. This leaves them loose and black and they must be discarded.

KILNING

After the log has been cut into boards on huge bandsaws (steel bands with sharp teeth on one edge), the boards must be dried. Not just cooked, or aired, but properly dried in ovens called KILNS. These are brick, or metal sheeted sheds, built to special design.

Kilns require heat, steam, and air circulation. The idea is to bring all parts of all boards to equal, and usable MOISTURE CONTENT. Moisture content is the proportion of moisture left in the wood compared to the true weight of the bone dry wood, and is expressed as a percentage.

The method of kilning is to stack all boards on trolleys, with sticks in between to allow air to circulate. The complete stack is rolled into the kiln and the airtight door is closed. Steam is now pumped into the kiln through holes in the floor. This steam circulates as it rises and is absorbed by the wood. When any surplus steam rises to the top it condenses and is extracted either by natural draught or by fans. Heating pipes maintain the kiln temperature during this moisture absorption period. Working to previously calculated schedule, the steam is gradually cut down and the heat is increased. Eventually the moisture in the wood starts to come out and is carried away as the air circulates.

In this way each board loses moisture at the same rate; evenly throughout its bulk. Any shrinkage that takes place is now even all through, and in good hands, very little distortion occurs. Boards are dried to a moisture content to match their eventual destination, be it garden fence, house timber, bedroom furniture or hospital furniture. The extent to which the kilning is carried out controls the future behaviour of the wood, for wood will always absorb atmospheric moisture in winter and give it up in summer, which is why doors stick at Christmas and windows rattle in a summer storm. This is why the schedules for drying try to induce stability by balancing moisture content against the future environment. Bedrooms are liable to be colder and not so dry as say hospital wards.

After kilning, the wood, which we now call TIMBER, must be protected against damp penetration, which is one of the reasons why you paint PRIMERS on to any finished joinery work. This keeps out moisture and provides a key for future paint. KNOTTING, a protective shellac, is painted over knots prior to priming. This seals the knot and prevents exuded resin marring the final paint.

MAN-MADE WOOD
Some wood from trees does not end up as board timber at all. It is processed to become sheet material to provide area cover rather than to give structural strength as does most carpentry timber.

Plywood
Logs are peeled on a machine with a long knife. The logs are mounted between centres and rotated against the knife. The peeled leaf of wood is called VENEER. Before this, the log is steamed or soaked in a pit to make it soft for cutting.

The veneer is clipped to remove defects and then dried. It is then assembled in sheet sizes and glued. After glueing, the veneer leaves are built up into a stack of layers, having the correct amount to suit the required finished thickness of the plywood to be made. Each intermediate layer is rotated through 90°. This gives plywood its immense strength and stability. There must always be an odd number of veneers to prevent distortion and to ensure matching grain direction on outer faces.

After glueing the stack is pressed in a hot press which sets the adhesive (glue) hard. The resulting board is strong, stable, and reasonably durable (long lasting). Special adhesives may make it water and boil proof. Insects will not attack such adhesives. If a veneer of decorative wood is now added there is the basis for a furniture panel.

Blockboard
BLOCKBOARDS are made from assembled wood strips bonded together when a thick veneer is glued to each face to make a sandwich. The strips of wood should not be more than 25mm (1 in.). Blockboards are not quite as stable as plywood, but are lighter and more easily worked.

Similar to blockboard is LAMINATED BOARD. These boards are basically the same as blockboard, but each strip, or lamination is limited to a maximum of 7 mm ($\frac{5}{16}$ in.). In this lies the board quality, for with strips as narrow as this any tendency to shrink or move is averaged out. LAMINBOARD (a trade name) is used for top quality work and is very expensive.

Another similar board to blockboard is BATTAN-BOARD. This is made with strips up to 75 mm (3 in.) wide. Each strip is crippled prior to assembly by having machine cut grooves made along its face. This reduces the strength of the batten and prevents it from moving sufficiently to move the whole board.

Particle Board
This is the most common of modern sheet material. Simply, a mass of particles are glued and then pressed together whilst the adhesive cures (sets).

The particles are wood chips, flax (which is the fibre of the *Linum* plant), or BAGASSE, which is the residue from the sugar cane after it is crushed for the sugar.

The most common of these, and the one likely to be used in carpentry, is the wood chip, and the board is called CHIPBOARD. Chipboard is lighter than either of the others and more stable.

The chips are specially prepared (cut) or they may be selected joinery factory waste, and then they are dried in hot air. They are then rotated into a mist of molten paraffin wax, which seals their surfaces and thus prevents undue absorption of the adhesive. This keeps cost and weight down and gives some degree of water resistance.

After the wax, the waterproof adhesive is fed in. The resulting sticky mass is then spread on to a flat platten and then pressed to board thickness and heated to cure the glue.

For a board to finish 18 mm ($\frac{3}{4}$ in.) in thickness the spread would be about 100 mm (4 in.). Boards may be made lighter still if fine chips are spread first, then coarse ones, and then a second layer of fine ones. This is called LAYER BOARD and it has a fine smooth surface.

GENERAL
A good craftsman studies his materials in order to achieve the best and most satisfying results in the most economic way. A piece of timber rejected for a bookshelf may well make back rails for a sink unit, and a ply panel taken out of a scrapped piece of furniture may later find use as a tool box lid.

Timber types are covered in Chapter 14.

2 Sawing to Size

SAW CUTTING THEORY

Sawing is to 'separate'. A board which has been one, becomes two. In practice the piece sawn off is usually waste and the remainder is the piece required. This thought is essential, for saws have thickness, and they remove wood. Note that our 'timber' has reverted to 'wood'. Sawn lengths bought at the yard are 'timber', but once they have been selected for use most people speak of the material as wood. Saws remove wood, and can spoil wood, right at the start of the job. After all, a board 150 mm wide (6 in.), will not make two strips at 75 mm (3 in.), so an allowance for saw wastage is essential. Thus the reminder to think of one piece as the work piece. Accordingly, when marking for cutting, the waste piece should be indicated by shading and the saw should be used to the waste side of the line. The line is left on. This entails careful saw control to cut just clear of the line and not on the line.

It is a good thing, also, to remember at planning stage, for when ordering wood, saw waste must be included and the job designed around standard width boards to minimise waste and saw cuts. Fig. 2 shows type of marking required.

HOW SAWS CUT

Saws cut because each tooth removes a small particle of wood as it travels along. Each tooth will remove the same size particle, and these particles, called saw dust, add up to a thin strip of wood removed. The thickness of this strip is the total width of the cut and this is called the saw KERF (see Fig. 2).

Wood has grain, which is the general lie of the wood fibre, and this runs along each board (or top to bottom of the tree). To cut these fibres across and to leave a clean sawn edge is a different job entirely to that of cutting them along their length. The first, cutting across, is called CROSS CUTTING, and the second, cutting along the board, is called RIPSAWING.

Saws are made from thin steel plates having triangular teeth along one edge. The tooth shape varies according to the type of cutting the saw has to do. From this it is evident that there must be a correct saw for use for each type of job. The saw type is determined by the shape of the saw, its handle, its plate and its tooth shape and size. More of this later.

Cross Cutting

To cut across the fibre, or grain, the saw teeth must be sharpened to needle points. Each tooth must sever the fibre cleanly and leave as few whiskers as possible. To give side clearance the teeth are SET. This means that half of the total number are sprung to one side, and the other half are sprung to the

Fig. 2.

a Mark out to avoid waste. Allow for thickness of saw cuts.

b Width of cut is called 'the kerf', side clearance is 'set'.

c Cut to waste side of line. Needle teeth for cross-cutting sever fibres cleanly.

d Rip-saw teeth cut material away chip-by-chip because of their 'chisel' edges.

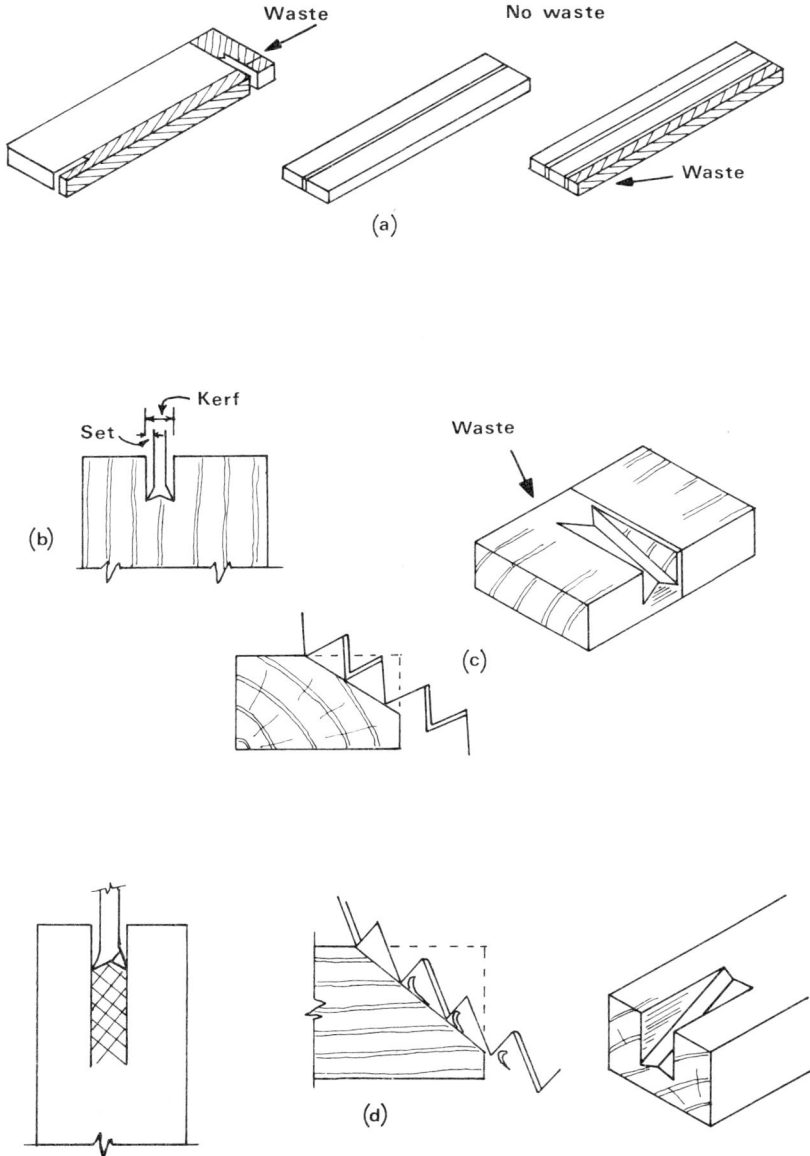

Waste   No waste

Waste

(a)

Kerf

Set

(b)

Waste

(c)

(d)

other side. Clearance is necessary to enable the saw to move freely in the cut, for wood is resilient, and under pressure it tends to compress, only to spring back again when pressure is relieved, thus closing in on the saw plate.

Each range of teeth for cross-cutting saws must cut a precise fine line into the wood. The material between these two lines is very short and is easily knocked out as the teeth pass, so cross-cutting teeth require no chisel, or cutting edges, other than their extreme needle tops (see Fig. 2). The process is rather like running two very sharp knife cuts close together across a board. The wood surface between the cuts falls easily away.

Ripsawing

Ripsawing requires something extra to the teeth. They must cut with a chisel action. Each tooth must remove by cutting, chip upon chip, along the board until the end is reached. Wood fibres are tightly bonded together and each fibre bundle must be chopped through. Chopping is wedging; this statement will be amplified in Chapter Three, where wood planing is explained.

Anyhow, rip teeth are chisel shaped. Each one leans more towards the wood than do cross-cutting teeth, and does not trail. Each one has a broad cutting edge, unlike the needle pointed tips of the cross-cutting tooth. The particles removed are larger than those of cross-cutting dust.

Ripsawing teeth are set to give side clearance, but are sharpened at different angles to cross-cutting teeth, and this produces the chisel edges required.

SAW TEETH

Saw teeth are triangular and vary in size and shape for each saw type. In general ripsawing teeth are more upright than cross-cutting teeth and have no bevel across their faces.

The precise angles to which saw teeth are sharpened are given later, in the section on *Saw Maintenance*.

SAW TYPES

Saws may be classified according to shape. Some classification is based on tooth shape, as is the position with tenon and dovetail saws, which look identical but are different in size. The three main classifications are:

Hand Saws, Back Saws, and *Shaping Saws.*

This last classification includes several rather special saws and the whole group may be thought of as MISCELLANEOUS saws. Handsaw outlines are shown in Fig. 3.

Fig. 3.

Ripsaws are from 660 mm to 710 mm long and have from 3 to 4 points per 25 mm.

Cross-cut saws are from 500 mm to 660 mm and have 5 to 8 points per 25 mm. Panel saws are from 460 mm to 610 mm and have 7 to 12 points per 25 mm.

The 'Nick' tooth is not often used and is rarely found on modern saws.

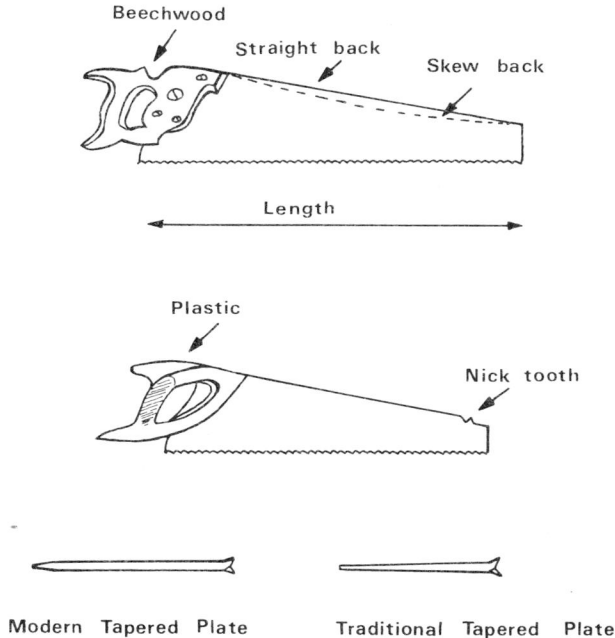

Beechwood

Straight back

Skew back

Length

Plastic

Nick tooth

Modern Tapered Plate   Traditional Tapered Plate

HAND SAWS

These saws are flat steel strips, with the width tapered in length. They have no means of rigidity other than the internal stresses set up by rolling during manufacture. Only if their teeth are kept sharp and their use skilful, will they perform well.

The three types are: RIPSAWS, CROSS-CUT saws and PANEL saws. Each has different teeth. The ripsaw runs from 610 mm to 710 mm long, (24 in. to 28 in.) and has fairly coarse, chisel-edged teeth. It is intended for rip-sawing along the grain only. The second, the cross-cut, runs from 520 mm to 710 mm long (22 in. to 28 in.), and has slightly smaller teeth than the rip-saw, and these are sharpened to needle points. Cross-cutting saws will cut along as well as across the grain, but not so well as will ripsaws. The third handsaw is the panel saw, and this is a saw for the woodworker who really desires to do his job well. Panel saws are shorter than rip or cross-cuts, and have finer teeth. They run in length from 405 mm to 520 mm (16 in. to 22 in.). The tooth angles lie between those of the rip and cross-cut. Panel saws may be used for cutting thin sheet material such as plywood and blockboard, and for cutting large tenons, in place of the tenon saw.

The handles of these saws are mainly of beechwood, with closed loop shape, but today many are being made of moulded plastic. At the same time as the tool designer re-models the handle, so he looks at the traditional tool shape, and many new saws have variations in both handle shape and blade shape. The main consideration is that they must be in 'in balance' and feel well.

Handsaw plate is of high carbon steel with some alloying elements of harder metal to give longer cutting life. The blade should be flexible, but tempered and tensioned to spring back straight if it is bent round and then released. The back edge may be straight or skewed, when it is hollowed in towards the toothed edge. Quality saws were once ground fully tapered in thickness across the saw plate from tooth to back, but today the most one can expect is for the back edge to have been pulled between two close-set grinding wheels to give a narrow edge of taper.

BACK SAWS

Back saws have backing strips of steel or (traditionally) brass, clamped tightly along their back edges. The backing strip serves two purposes. Firstly, the heavier and thicker back strip prevents the saw from bending due to excessive cutting force, and secondly it provides a means of keeping the tooth edge in tension. By pinching tightly to the saw plate it is able to stretch the saw plate as it itself is stretched. Thus if the tooth edge of a back saw starts to waver and is felt to be 'loose', i.e. extra flexible but without much resilience, it can be made taut if the back strip is struck a few smart taps with a hammer along its back edge. This tends to stretch it and bow it towards the saw plate, thus stretching the tooth edge. The back saws are: the TENON saw, from 305 mm to 405 mm long, and used for larger joint cutting; the DOVETAIL saw, from 205 mm to 255 mm long, used for fine limit cutting such as for the cutting of close-fitting joints; and the LIGHT BACK saw, which is made very light, as short as 100 mm, and in longer versions up to 800 mm long. This saw has a turned, in-line handle. It is used for cutting very fine beads, and slender work generally.

All of this group of saws have much finer plate and teeth than have hand saws, and because they are used at all angles to the grain, all have needle point teeth.

THE TENSIONED SAWS

These are: the BOW saw, the COPING saw, and the FRET saw. In each, the saw is thin and narrow and is held in tension by either a twisted string for the bow saw, or by the springiness of the steel frame in the coping and fret saw. The purpose of these saws is to cut shapes in wood, but they may also be used on rigid plastic, brass or aluminium sheet. For penetrated shapes, a hole is first bored and the saw is threaded through before it is sprung and screwed into its frame. To avoid bending or breaking these fine saws, they must be held square to their line of cut. With bow saws and coping saws, the saw blade may be rotated in its frame to secure the easiest approach to the cut.

PAD ór KEYHOLE SAWS

These saws are intended for aperture work only. The blade is stiff and is held into a turned wooden handle, or cast metal handle, by screws. Holes are first bored and then the saw is inserted to cut. As the cut proceeds more of the saw may be inserted and a longer cutting stroke used.

The saw teeth of all the above shaping saws are filed square across to chisel edges. Fret saw blades are not usually re-sharpened but are considered disposable. (They are useful though, to keep as long, thin, probes should a tiny screw etc. be lost in a confined space such as a door lock.)

Of the above saws, all work with a pushing action, with teeth pointing away from the handle, except for the fret which has its teeth pulled into the work by the handle. The coping saw may have its blade pushed, or pulled, depending on whether the cut is horizontal or vertical.

COMPASS SAWS

These are sets of flat, tapered blades, each one having teeth suitable for a different job. Generally the set consists of a long, wide blade (about 50 mm or 2 in. wide at widest part) suitably toothed for shaping large curves in wood; a shorter, very narrow blade for use as a keyhole saw, and another wide blade toothed with very coarse, spiky teeth, for tree pruning. These blades all fit into a standard open hook saw handle. Fig. 4 shows the bow-saw, coping saw, fret saw, pad saw and compass saw in use.

SAW TEETH

To re-cap: Ripsaw teeth have chisel edges to remove wood, but all others (other than the tensioned saws) have needle points. This is because ripsaws cut only along the grain whereas all others cut grain at any angle. Saw teeth are illustrated in detail in Fig. 5.

SAW MAINTENANCE

Saws must be protected from rust by a film of oil, best wiped from an oily rag pad. Their teeth must be protected from contact with steel or stone, either by protective grooved wood strips, or by careful hanging when not in use.

Fig. 4.
a Bowsaws have beech frames and the saws are held in tension by string tourniquets.
b Coping saws have their blades held in tension by screw action as the handle is rotated.
c Fretsaw blades are held in tension by the springiness of the saw frame.
d Pad, or keyhole, saws have stiff blades and are ideal for small apertures.
e Compass saw blades are stiff and have teeth shaped to suit varying requirements.

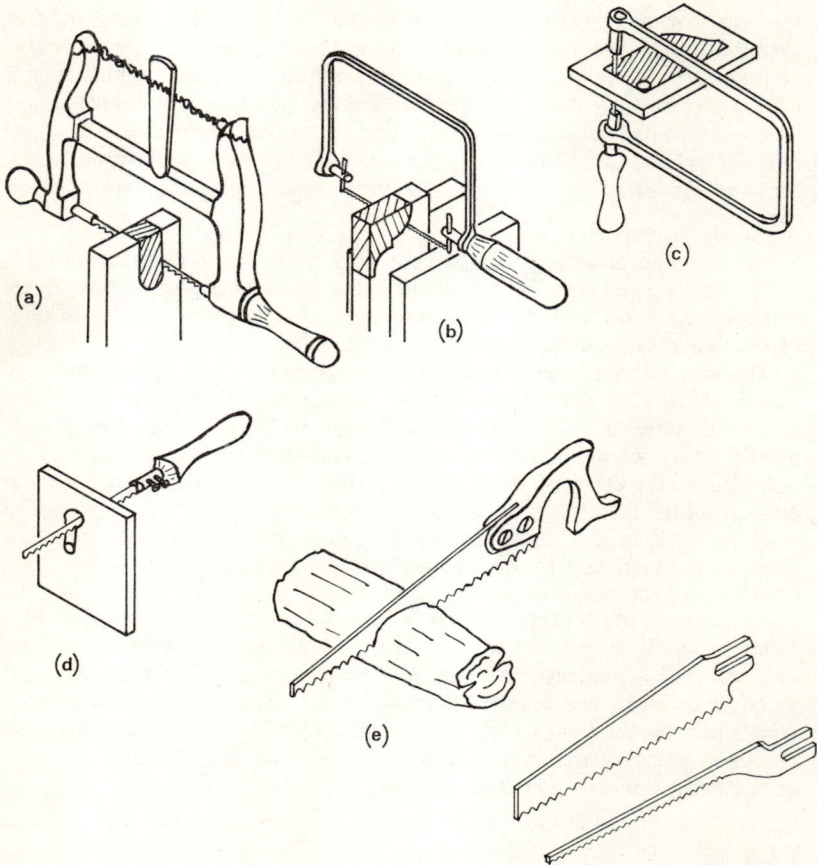

(a)

(b)

(c)

(d)

(e)

Saw teeth are filed to sharpness, and all may be re-sharpened (apart from coping and fret blades). Filing is a delicate, highly skilled job best left to the expert. However, no man with respect for his tools will be content not to try this job. Remember though, a good saw may be ruined by continuous poor filing. However, every competent wood worker has the potential to learn the job by practice, given a few pieces of equipment.

A saw filing vice, or horse is necessary. It may be as simple as two bevelled wood strips clamped to either side of the saw, or it may be a complete, free standing tool used for this one job only. Its essential job is to

Fig. 5.
a Ripsaw teeth have bevelled tops and square faces.
b Cross-cut teeth have bevelled tops and faces, and lean back. Cross-cutting saws have 5 to 8 points per 25 mm. Tenon saws have 12 to 14 points per 25 mm. Dovetail saws have 18 to 22 points per 25 mm. Fine Back saws have 16 to 32 points per 25 mm.

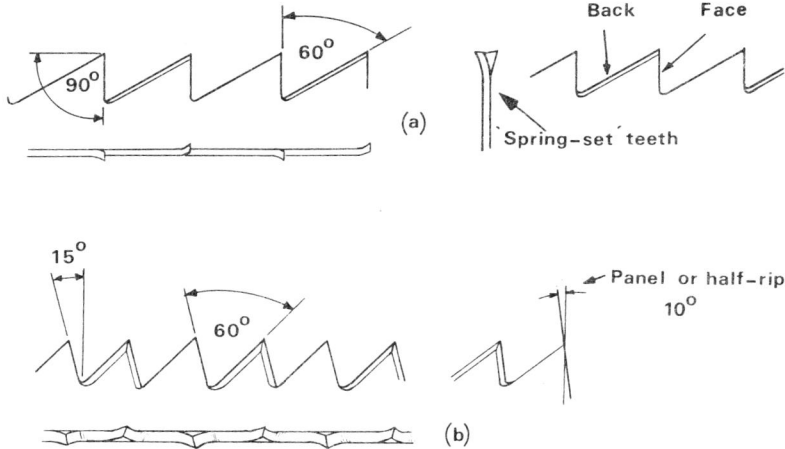

clamp closely to the saw teeth to hold them against the cut of the file. The problems of saw holding are that hand saws are very wide at the handle, and that back saws have thick back strips. Some experiment is necessary to see how the saws to be filed may be held in the equipment available. Use may be made of the standard bench vice or of the standard engineer's vice. The saw tooth line should be approximately level with the filer's elbow.

The files used are TAPER SAW FILES which are slender files, triangular in section, tapered in length, and having single-cut file teeth, with rounded corners. They may be single-ended, with a tang or be double-ended for further use. They may be bought as 'slim-section' for fine tooth work, or standard for handsaws. Sometimes they are called 'THREE SQUARE FILES'.

Metal working files have double-cut file teeth and have sharp corners. Files are sold by length of blade, which is usually related to size of cross-section; shorter files being smaller in cross-section than longer ones. For most handsaws, 150 mm (6 in.) files will do, or even, if large teeth are found, files of 200 mm (8 in.). For dove-tail and small tenon saws, 100 mm (4 in.) slim-section files must be used.

The best technique is to follow existing angles and to sharpen before the saw is blunt. A light touch is all that is required. Pressure is only exerted on the forward stroke, but the file is kept in contact on the draw-back stroke. Two strokes on each tooth should be sufficient for any saw. For all saws the file is held horizontal. The variable angles are the angle of the file line across the saw, and the angle to which the file is rotated to give the correct face hook angle to the tooth. FACE HOOK is the angle at which the face, or cutting edge of a tooth, is inclined away from the cutting line.

Every other tooth is filed from one side, filing the face of one tooth and the back of the next in one stroke. When the end of the saw is reached the saw is reversed for the remaining half to be filed.

If the saw has been badly treated by poor filing or nail cutting, the technique is to first RANGE the teeth. This means that a flat file is lightly run along the tooth line, bringing all, or most of, the teeth back into a common line. The saw is then laid flat and the same file is gently rubbed along to even out uneven side set.

Should there be kinks or bends in the saw these are treated by light hammering. An old flat-iron, held sole up in a vice, is covered with a thin card. Any saw lumps are very lightly knocked down on this, the cardboard allowing the distorted metal to bend back into shape. Only very light hammering is permissible; anything else will tend to stretch the tooth edge and make it wavy.

Setting
This means giving side clearance to the saw blade by side-springing the teeth. Half go to one side, half go to the other. The amount of side clearance depends on the saw type, the saw condition and the wood being cut. Large saws required more set than small ones, old saws that tend to have kinks and lumps require more set than new ones, and saws used for soft wet wood require more set than those used on dry, hard woods. By far the largest number of home and professional woodworkers use SAW PLIERS, a mechanical tool that springs over a saw tooth each time its jaws are closed by hand pressure. Its essentials are a punch, and an anvil. The punch bends the tooth and the anvil control the limit of bend, thus controlling the amount of set. The anvil is adjustable to varying requirements of set. To generalise, if the saw is held across the face, with the saw back edge towards the eyes, set should be noticeable along the tooth line. An obtrusive jagged line indicates too much set.

After setting, a very light side range with the flat file will ensure regularity.

A saw doctor will be necessary if the saw becomes too loose. This means that it has lost its tension, and will rattle in the cut as it is drawn back, or will bend as forward force is applied. It will also rattle if shaken. This condition is due to prolonged use and frequent filing. The cure is by hammer or by roller. The centre section or band must be rolled or hammer-stretched until it creates a tensional force along the back and tooth edges. This force is the force that keeps handsaw plates flat and stiff in use.

SAW USE

All saws must cut their way into the wood. Sufficient force must be applied to enable teeth to bite, but no more than this, for undue force will bend the saw plate.

The saw must become an extension of the arm, directed by eye, and it must move in a free-flowing movement. The handle must be gripped with three fingers and thumb, with the forefinger resting straight along side of handle and pointing into cut.

At the start of the cut the saw is drawn back, thus giving an entrance path for the teeth when they are then pushed forward. To guide the saw at this stage, the left hand grips the work, with the ball or side of its thumb resting against the saw blade as a guide.

The wood must be firmly held by hand, knee, or vice, and positioned to give best body movement. Large panels, or long boards should be rested on two carpenters stools, which are simple wood trestles. By kneeling with one knee on the wood the necessary hold-down force is given. For really heavy rip cutting, the sawyer may sit astride the board and use the saw two handed, with the teeth either towards, or away from him.

Shorter boards may be best held upright in the bench vice.

For joint cutting the BENCH HOOK is used. This is a simple board of about 22mm ($\frac{7}{8}$ in.) thick by 250 mm (10 in.) long and about 150 mm (6 in. wide). At both ends, but at opposing sides, there is an end stop which makes the board into a hook. With the end stops perfectly square to the board, it is easy to hold and to cut accurately any necessary cuts for joint forming.

3 Taking the Rough to the Smooth

HAND PLANES AND PLANING

To make 'plane' is to make flat. In a horizontal plane no part of the surface is higher or lower than any other part. The woodworker aims to make all of his surfaces 'plane' surfaces, but the nature of wood being what it is, prone to move in shape as it gains or loses moisture, this aim is not easily accomplished. So the woodworker compromises. He settles for a seemingly flat surface and only asks that it be smooth to touch and able to accept a final protective smooth and decorative finish.

All work from the saw has saw marks throughout its surface. It may well be, in general, flat, but to the touch it is rough—so it must be planed. Furthermore, it will vary in size, as sawing is not expected to be finely accurate, and has to be 'planed' to size, as well as smoothed. These then, are the jobs of the 'plane': smoothing and sizing.

CUTTING ACTION OF PLANES

All cutting is chopping, and all chopping is wedging. This statement is true of all, or nearly all, woodworking cutting tools. The thin end of the wedge is inserted by force. The thicker part follows, and before we know it the grain line is riven and pieces have separated. The sharp penetrating edge of the chopper does not contact the wood after it has penetrated. Wood fibres are torn asunder by the wedge shape of the chopper head following its sharp edge. But this will not do for the woodworker; he requires a smooth finish.

So planes were invented, improved on, and are now sold as sophisticated tools able to do perfect work.

The sole, or base, of the plane is flat. About one third along from its leading end, or toe, there is a mouth through which the plane iron projects. The sharp projecting end of the iron points into the wood surface. A thin skim, or shaving, is torn away and vanishes up through the mouth and along the face of the iron. Now wood has grain, and this wanders and undulates throughout the length of the board, so the shaving varies in thickness as the riving end attempts to follow the grain line. The resulting surface will be something less than truly flat and will not be accepted as smooth. So the plane iron is fitted with a CAP IRON, which fits tight and snug to the plane iron face, just short of the extreme cutting edge. The shaving now meets the cap iron and is abruptly turned away. It cracks and weakens. But a tough and resistant shaving will curl and not crack and be able to pull more and more wood fibres out to support itself. The surface is still left rough. So the edge of the mouth is brought close in. Now we have the ideal tool; a plane that will, depending on the setting (or projection) of the iron, skim a thick or a thin shaving and leave a silky smooth surface.

The above reasoning is illustrated in Fig. 6.

Fig. 6.

a All cutting is chopping. A chopping edge rives material due to the wedging action of the cutting edge.

b A plane iron acts as a wedge and tears. Without a 'cap-iron' the tear will follow the line of the grain.

c The 'cap-iron' acts as the body of the wedge and turns the shaving sufficiently for it to crack as it curls. With a wide plane mouth the tear will still go deeply into the grain.

d With close-set cap iron and narrow mouth, the shaving cracks easily and is no longer strong enough to tear grain away.

e The correctly curled shaving will show fine cracks.

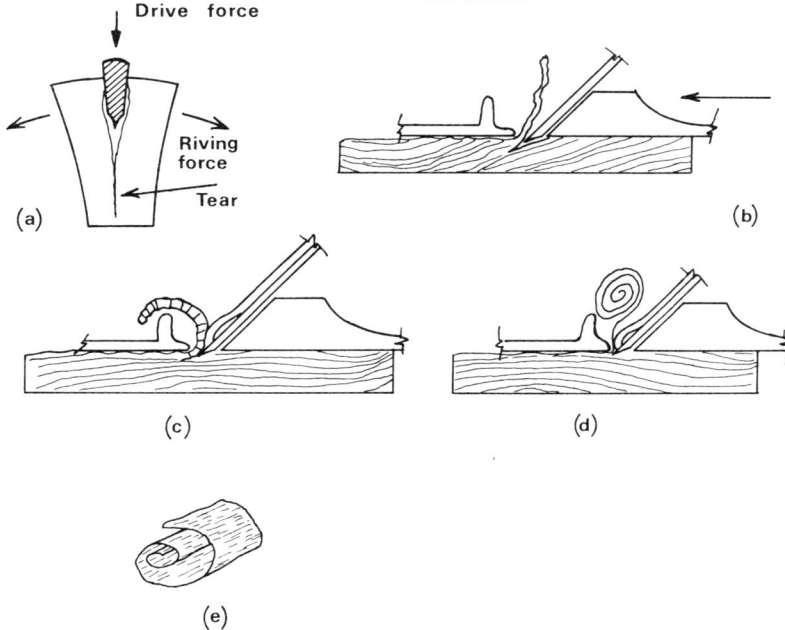

PRINCIPLES OF PLANE DESIGN

The plane is used to make flat the wood surface. To do this it is rested on the surface and pushed forward. The plane sole is flat and if its length is sufficient to span the worst of the variations in surface, its path will be straight and the wood will be left straight. In practice it is not quite as simple as this. The woodworker must assess the surface by eye to pick out the high spots and then use the plane to cut away these high spots until all is flat.

In describing the plane, it was said that the iron projects below the sole. This is so, and this fact makes it necessary for the user to learn to use the plane with skill. The fore-part of the plane sole rests on the wood. The iron follows it and theoretically the wood becomes flat. But as the iron travels along it leaves a gap, fine, but still a gap, between the planed surface and the tail end of the plane sole. So the plane dips; its nose goes up and its tail down. It has changed its direction and no change in direction is possible in a flat surface or straight line. In general, then, the work surface tends to be planed slightly hollow. Another factor creeps in here; that of user skill or non-skill. The plane design tends to alleviate the non-skill of the user, for as the toe is placed on the work the longer tail part tends to drop and to make the work round (in length). At the last end of the wood, the reverse occurs. The toe drops. The result is still the same; the surface planed tends to be round. These factors then—the tendency of the plane, inherent in its design, to plane hollow—is balanced by the contradictory tendency of the user to plane round. Thus, with reasonable skill, the woodworker is able to plane two edges to fit, to make a joint between long boards. Fig. 7 shows the principle of straight line planing.

THE PLANES

To enable plane design to be effectively used, three sizes of planes are produced. Although each 'size' plane is produced in varying sizes, it is possible to recognise a plane from its size. The sizes are grouped as follows:

Try or *Jointer*	For long, flat planing. 560 mm to 610 mm (22 in. to 24 in.).
Jack	For general bench working. 300 mm. to 375 mm ($11\frac{1}{2}$ in. to 15 in.).
Smoothing	For careful finishing. 180 mm to 259 mm ($5\frac{3}{4}$ in. to 10 in.) prior to sanding

The IRONS of all the above planes are of high carbon steel. This will hold a fine sharp edge over a long period. The name 'iron', is a relic of the past but has become accepted as the correct technical name for the plane cutting-tool.

In addition to the length variation, bench planes vary in cutting width. The try planes have irons of either 60 mm or 66 mm wide ($2\frac{3}{8}$ in. to $2\frac{5}{8}$ in.). The jack planes have irons of 44 mm, 50 mm or 56 mm wide ($1\frac{3}{4}$ in., 2 in., or $2\frac{1}{4}$ in.). The smoothing planes have irons 41 mm, 44 mm, 50 mm and 60 mm wide ($1\frac{5}{8}$ in., $1\frac{3}{4}$ in., 2 in., and $2\frac{3}{8}$ in.).

As each of the above is intended for special applications so the cutting angle of each is special to its particular job. Try planes and jack planes have pitch angles of 46°, but the smoothing planes have a lower angle of 44°. The iron pitch is the angle contained between the face of the iron and the sole of the plane.

Other Planes

There are very many small and special planes. Only four of these merit inclusion with bench planes for they are similar in design and approximate use. They are the: COMPASS plane, the SHOULDER plane, the BULLNOSE plane, and the BLOCK plane. Each is used to plane flat shavings.

Fig. 7.
a To make surface flat, high spots are removed first.
b The projecting plane iron tends to make work 'hollow'.
c The tendency for the heel to drop and toe to rise as cutting stroke begins, is reversed as it finishes; this tends to produce 'round' work. The two tendencies cancel each other out and allow perfectly straight work to be achieved.
d Short planes ride the bumps, long planes span them.
c A change in pressure from start to finish of each stroke helps the plane design to give a straight cut.

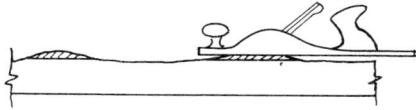

(a)

Toe ↑   ↓ Heel

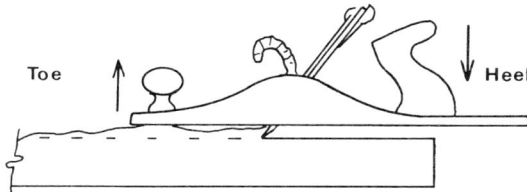

(b)

(c)

(d)

Press down   Press down

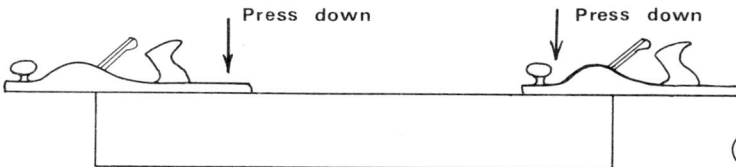

(e)

The compass plane has the same iron and cap iron as the smoothing plane, but its sole plate is flexible, and by adjustment, may be made concave or convex to fit any curved edge that requires planing.

The shoulder plane is intended for planing across the grain to enable adjustment to previously cut joint shoulders. It will, of course cut and plane along the grain as well, and this makes it very useful for final cleaning of rabbets and wide grooves that have been cut by other means.

It has a solid body and differs from the previous planes in that the iron is as wide as the body (i.e. cuts into corners) and that it, the iron, is placed in the plane, face side down. This is called REVERSE angle. It has no front handle but is comfortably held in one hand for use.

The pitch of the shoulder plane is low, as low as 16°. In width it varies from 12 mm to 35 mm ($\frac{1}{2}$ in. to $1\frac{3}{8}$ in.).

The bullnose plane is similar in principle to the shoulder plane but is shorter and broader. It has a reverse angle iron and a very low pitch from 12° to 18°. It is useful for cleaning the ends of stopped rabbets and for cleaning bevelled work. A very useful feature of bullnose plane design is that the portion of its body in front of the iron may be removed, enabling planing into an abrupt corner. Its width varies from 18 mm to 32 mm ($\frac{3}{4}$ in. to $1\frac{1}{4}$ in.).

The block plane is small and is a reverse angle plane. It has a solid sole and the iron projects through a mouth. The cap iron is a casting and continues beyond the cutting iron, where it is shaped for convenient grasp. It is the general purpose 'finishing and fitting' plane, able to cut across end grain, cut across wild, woolly, and interlocked grain, and, moreover, able to be used in cramped positions of space. It is about 150 mm long by cutting width of 38 mm (6 in. × $1\frac{1}{2}$ in.), and has a low pitch of 12° to 18°.

MAINTENANCE OF PLANES AND IRONS

Plane irons must be sharp. Blunt irons produce poor work and absorb a lot of energy that could be more usefully employed. To keep a fine edge means adequate sharpening. The iron starts its life blunt. It comes from the plane maker with its edge ground to a fine line and at the correct angle. It will be polished at the face and its edge will be square with its side; but it will not be sharp.

So our first step with a new plane is to put it in order. We can assume that the FROG, the angled casting on which the iron rests, is fitted correctly, and we can assume that the 'Y' adjusting lever and screw are in order, so that they will move the iron forward or back to increase, or decrease, the cut. The LATERAL ADJUSTING LEVER will also be in order, and capable of moving the iron sideways to line up its edge with the plane of the sole. The

LEVER CAP, which uses an eccentric lever to clamp the iron and cap iron into place will be working well. The handles will be rigid and all other screws tight.

It leaves us only three jobs: to degrease by washing with methylated spirit or paraffin; to sharpen the iron, and to SET the iron. Setting means the fitting of the iron and cap iron together and the assembly of them into the plane.

After degreasing for convenience in handling, a light rub of oil should be put back on all bright parts. (Except those chromium plated). The iron is released from its cap by slackening the centre screw and pivoting the iron sideways. It is then slid along until the large hole at the end of its slot will allow it to lift away.

Assume here that the iron has been used, re-sharpened, and used again, with an accidental contact with a hidden nail producing a gap or nick in the cutting edge.

A small bench grinder with a 'soft' cutting wheel is able to grind the iron. A 'hard' wheel will tend to burn out the carbon and spoil the tool. Grinding wheel technology is complex and beyond the scope of this book.

The correct angle at which to grind lies between 25° and 30°. This gives the most suitable clearance and holding power to the edge.

This angle is the angle between the line of the iron face and the line of the ground surface. The tool-rest should be set to give the chosen angle and the iron is passed to and fro across the wheel with light contact. Cool the iron frequently, or rather, wet it frequently to prevent it ever becoming other than cool. Carbon burns at grinding temperatures. Carbon is the hardness factor in the plane iron. Burning reduces the carbon in the edge and thus the edge-holding properties of the iron are lost.

When the bevel is about twice the length of the iron thickness the angle is about right. Keep grinding until the sparks coming over the wheel skate on down the iron face. At this stage you will know that the edge is sufficiently thin to carry on with the next process, that of sharpening.

An important point to remember when using a grinder is to protect your eyes with a face shield or goggles. Further, all small power tools need constant checking for loose bolts and screws, and for cable condition.

Irons are now sharpened on a bench oilstone, which is a manufactured block of abrasive, which uses an oil film to lubricate the contact between iron and stone and also to float away the small particles of steel that wear from the edge of the iron.

The whole of the ground bevel is now HONED, the name given to oilstone sharpening (WETTING is an alternative name). Only the extreme tip of the ground bevel is rubbed to and fro along the stone with the iron held ap-

Fig. 8.

a With tool rest pivoted, the correct angle of 25° to 30° is easily achieved.
b If the bevel is twice the iron thickness the angle is about right.
c Keep iron moving across the wheel. When sparks pass along down iron face, the edge has been ground to correct thickness.

d Constant checks for squareness are required.
e Oil abrasive stone and use all of its surface.
f Remove burr, keeping iron flat down.
g Hone edge between 30 and 35 degrees.

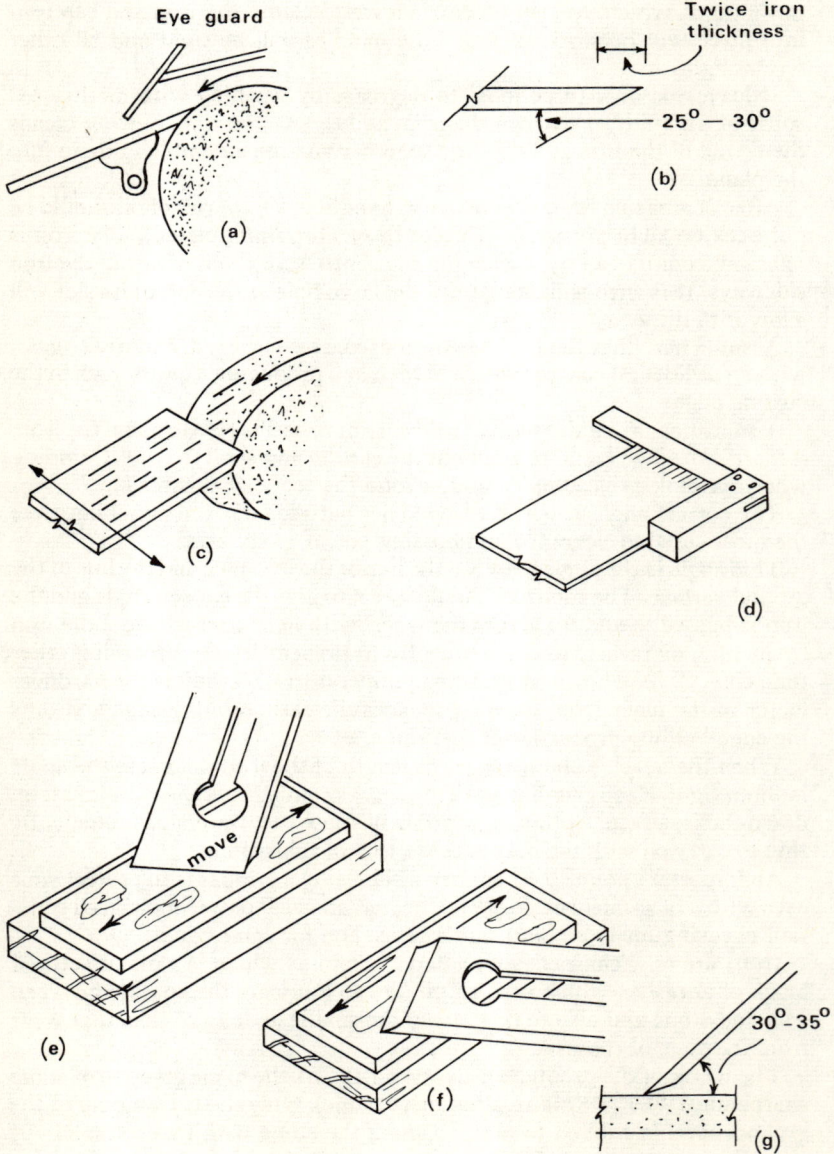

Eye guard

(a)

Twice iron thickness

25° — 30°

(b)

(c)

(d)

move

(e)

(f)

30° – 35°

(g)

Fig. 9.
a Maximum set-back for cap is 1.5 mm.
b Sight along sole to see edge of iron as a fine black line.
c Round corners of a jack-plane iron to avoid tracks on work.
d By advancing the 'Frog', the gap may be closed. Use coarse gaps for quick jacking and fine gaps for smoothing.

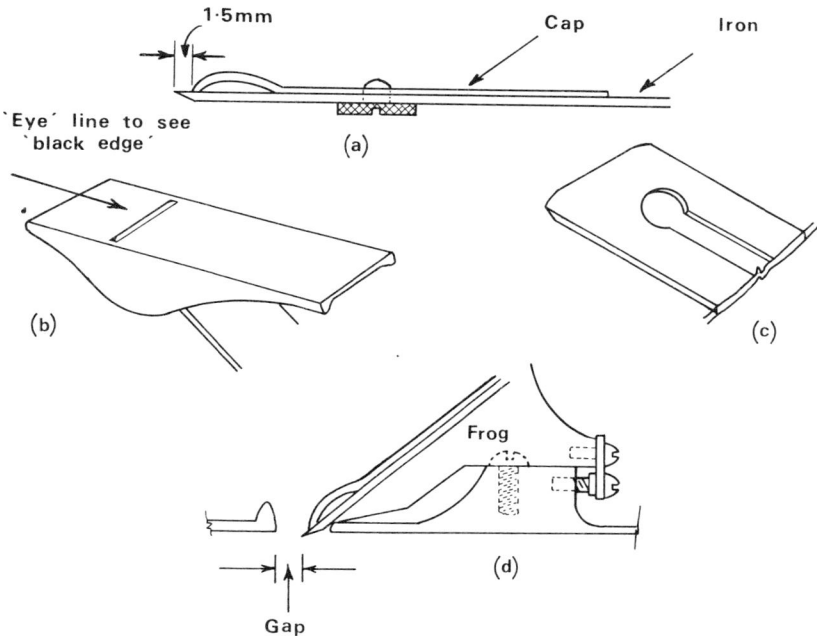

proximately at $30°/35°$ to the stone face. When a wire edge or burr is felt on the face, the iron is laid flat and a few rubs remove this burr.

For really keen edges the process is repeated on a finer stone.

When sharp, the iron is wiped dry and fitted to the cap iron, taking care that no contact is made between the end of the cap iron and the sharp cutting edge. Set the cap edge close to the sharp edge—say 1.5 mm away for general work or closer still for planing curly grained hardwood—and tighten screw. Insert iron and cap into plane and feel that the lateral lever is in correct contact by moving it from side to side. Slide on the lever cap and snap cap closed. The iron should now be firmly held.

Reverse plane and sight along sole from toe end. A thin hair-like black line should show for the iron edge. If not, correct setting by advancing or retarding the adjusting nut. If one edge is higher than the other use the lateral adjusting lever for correction.

Refinements of setting are necessary should wide boards of curly grain require planing.

Take out the iron and using the bench oilstone, slightly round the extreme corners of the cutting edge. This prevents overlap marks. Then release frog screws and adjust frog forward until the minimum gap necessary is left for chip escapement. Tighten all screws; re-assemble the plane and test, the shaving should be almost feather like, with a lacy appearance. A rub with a wax candle on the plane sole will complete the job started by the tool designer.

Figs. 8 and 9 illustrate the above points of plane maintenance.

4 Marking for Making

JOB DESIGN, MEASURING, MARKING AND TOOLS USED

As the tree grows from a small seed, so grows the wood project. The idea is born; out of a search for novelty, for change, or for basic living room. The idea is the beginning. Next comes the study for feasibility. What would such a thing cost? How should it be made? Where would it go? And how would it be fixed and finished?

Assuming that the idea has proved possible (to the awakened imagination) the practicalities have to be considered. How much space is available and how much material will be required? Later still: how is it to be made?

In this chapter, 'Design' as such is not dealt with, only the methods by which a pre-conceived design may be brought to reality.

A storage unit is required and it must be fixed into a recess between wall and chimney breast. Then we need to measure. The overall dimension of the opening is important. So also is a knowledge of the actual space available. The two are not necessarily the same. Ceilings and floors may be out of level. Walls may lean in, or out. Angles may be more, or less, than RIGHT ANGLES (90°).

To check all this we need two long, thin laths, called PINCH-RODS. These must be at least longer than half the opening size, but not longer than the minimum opening size. By gripping the two together in one hand and sliding them out until they fit into the opening, a measure of width or height may be obtained.

In practice, a BUILDER'S LEVEL is essential, for pinch-rods will give a parallel measure even to grossly sloping walls.

The pinch-rods are used in conjunction with the level, and a maximum rectangular opening is ascertained. Where the two rods pass each other in the hand, a pencil mark is made. This is for maximum and minimum height, and maximum and minimum width. The level will indicate the degree to which floors, ceilings and walls deviate from true level and plumb. A plumb bob, which is any small weight on the end of a fine string, is another essential, better even than the 'level' for checking the amount by which a wall slopes, in, or out.

The aim is to fit into the available area an accurately square unit. The margins will be SCRIBED at fitting stage. Scribing is the process of fitting one thing to another.

THE DRAWING

Having ascertained maximum size for height and width, these figures must be recorded. For the job mentioned (a recess storage unit), a strip of wood is all that is necessary. The tradesman woodworker will use a floorboard, a sheet of plywood or hardwood, or even a roll of lining paper. This will be called a ROD, which is the record of working instruction for all the job dimensions. The home carpenter may jot sizes down and purchase the main timber for the frame. The rod may then be marked on these. A 'height' rod and 'width' rod are essential. Working in from the datum points fixed, the widths of the outside members are drawn in. These must be sufficiently broad enough to allow enough strength in the chosen joints. Furthermore, if the design calls for these members to be the scribing pieces as well, rather than to have extra pieces planted on after construction, a very full allowance must be made. For the cupboard outlined, the two vertical members and the top horizontal member may be ex 75 mm by 25 mm (3 in. × 1 in.)—EX means 'Out of' which is the sawing size. The planing size may be about 70 mm × 20 mm. (2¾ in. × $\frac{13}{16}$ in.).

A HEIGHT rod, and a WIDTH rod are then drawn. These are vertical and horizontal sections (cut through) of the front frame of the job.

Next step is to make a list showing the complete amount of wood required. At this point it is essential to remember that timber yards work to standard sizes. 75 mm by 25 mm (3 in. × 1 in.) sawn will not be quite that. The width will have been sawn from a board 150 mm wide (6 in.) and the thickness from a board 50 mm (2 in.) thick. Thus the sawn piece will be about 73 mm × 23 mm and the strip bought planed will be about 70 mm × 20 mm (2¾ in. × $\frac{13}{16}$ in.). This problem of nominal size and actual size, must be reconciled with the rod, for it affects the distances between shoulders etc.

When all material has been selected, it is MARKED OUT. All the cuts that have to be made should be carefully marked. If some of the wood is bought sawn, it must be planed to size before marking.

MARKING OUT
Select best faces and edges. Mark these. Pair-up any work that must be HANDED. Think of your right and left hands, clap them together and then lay them out flat and this will help you to visualize handed work.

Best wood goes in maximum exposure area, with worst parts concealed, either above, or below, sight area. If any shape or taper is planned, defects must be arranged so that they are cut away in the process.

Shoulder sizes, the measure between two pieces that have another jointed in between, are marked directly from the rod. Overall heights and widths are marked, with waste that is to be cut away, crossed all over. Joint designs are marked out and then marked closely, with all waste wood crossed.

If work is being done that requires some solid moulding, then this too must be marked. Only if all subsequent cutting is marked clearly will the final job go together correctly. This marking out stage is often neglected, and often the job arrives at finishing stage with two right hands because of this neglect. Marking out enables ideas to be fully visualized (and changed if necessary) and if the original job measurement has been carefully incorporated in the working rod the final product will be of correct size. A point to remember is that of accessibility of job position. An 'across-the-room' cupboard unit could be designed and made in the garage, but then not be manoeuvrable up the stairs, and perhaps not even assembled in the bedroom. Such a job must be made in units. Central heating pipes, skirtings and picture rails should all be allowed for at rod stage. If they are not, the job just will not go in. Figs 10 and 11 show typical marking out.

THE TOOLS USED
The tools used for marking out consist of rules, squares, bevel, gauges, marking knife and dividers. Plus, of course, fine pointed pencils of perhaps HH grade, which is reasonably hard.

The rules required could be two in number, with perhaps a third added as a refinement.

First, you require a three-fold rule in either boxwood or plastic, with clearly legible figures. This may be either 610 mm (24 in.) or 1 metre 39·75 in. The shorter rule is more easily handled. This is the general purpose rule, for measuring and working.

Next, a two metre flexible tape rule provides a means of avoiding the use of a pinch-rod, but it does mean that figures must be recorded, rather than the simple pencil line used across the pinch rods. The steel tape is useful too, for measuring around curves for hardboard work. The better types of these steel tapes have markings in metric and imperial, and are marked on both faces. The face on the back of the tape is calibrated to give the direct measurement if the rule is unrolled between two walls.

The third rule is one for very accurate marking, and for setting the points on marking gauges and dividers. It is a 305 mm (12 in.) steel rule that has metric readings to one edge and imperial to the other. thus giving an easy means of conversion of units. This flat, straight rule is very useful for use as a short straight edge for straight line marking. Direct reading from the end makes measuring for rebate depths etc. very simple. Fig. 12 indicates uses of marking tools.

The Squares
The two squares required are the TRY square and the MITRE square. The first, the try square, has a rigid blade, best callibrated, set into a cast metal

Fig. 10.

a 'Face' and 'Edge' marks will create pairs if used correctly.

b Parts may be numbered if this is felt necessary.

c A working rod shows all heights, widths and shoulder sizes.

d A frame fitted to a poor wall will need tapered packing and scribed architraves.

c All mortises and waste are shown on the stile as it is marked out.

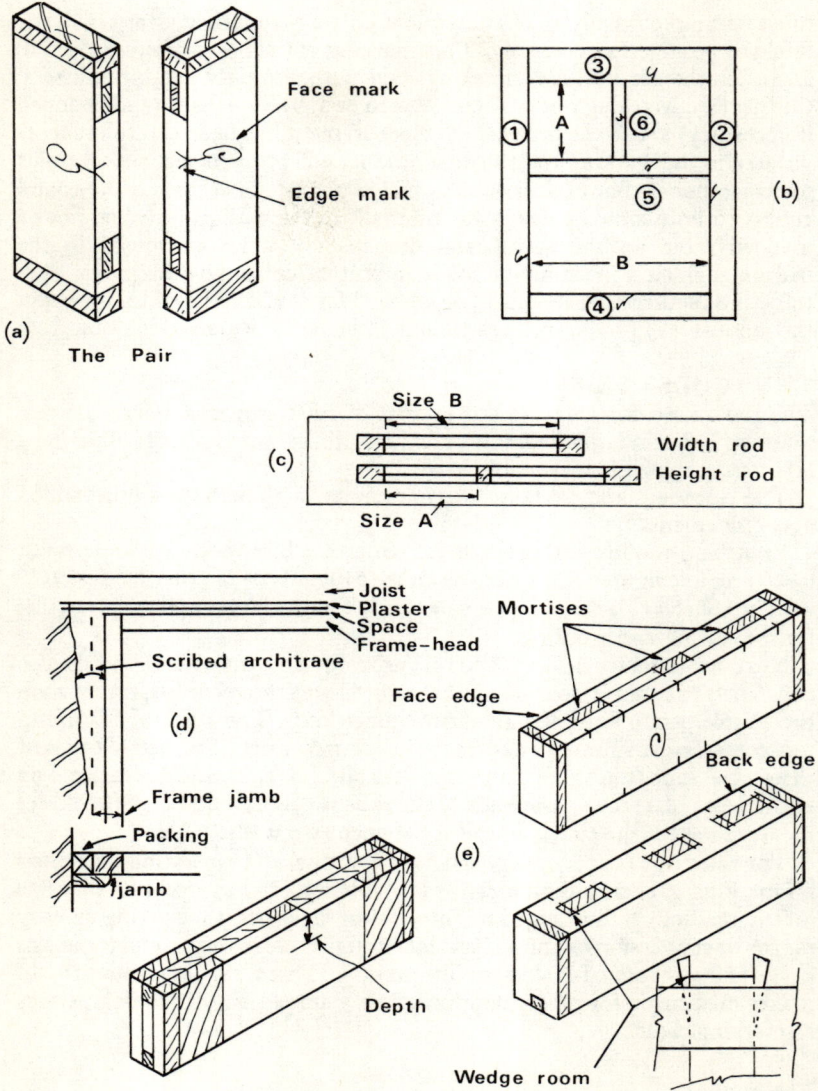

(a)

Face mark

Edge mark

The Pair

(b)

A

B

(c)

Size B

Width rod

Height rod

Size A

Joist
Plaster
Space
Frame-head

Scribed architrave

(d)

Frame jamb

Packing

jamb

Mortises

Face edge

Back edge

(e)

Depth

Wedge room

Fig. 11.

a As much information as necessary is given when marking out. Chamfer lines are pencilled, rabbet lines are gauged.

b Gauged lines will spoil chamfers. Rabbets need cut lines.

c Full marking for half-lap and table foot are shown.

d The dovetailed socket would only be marked from the finished tail.

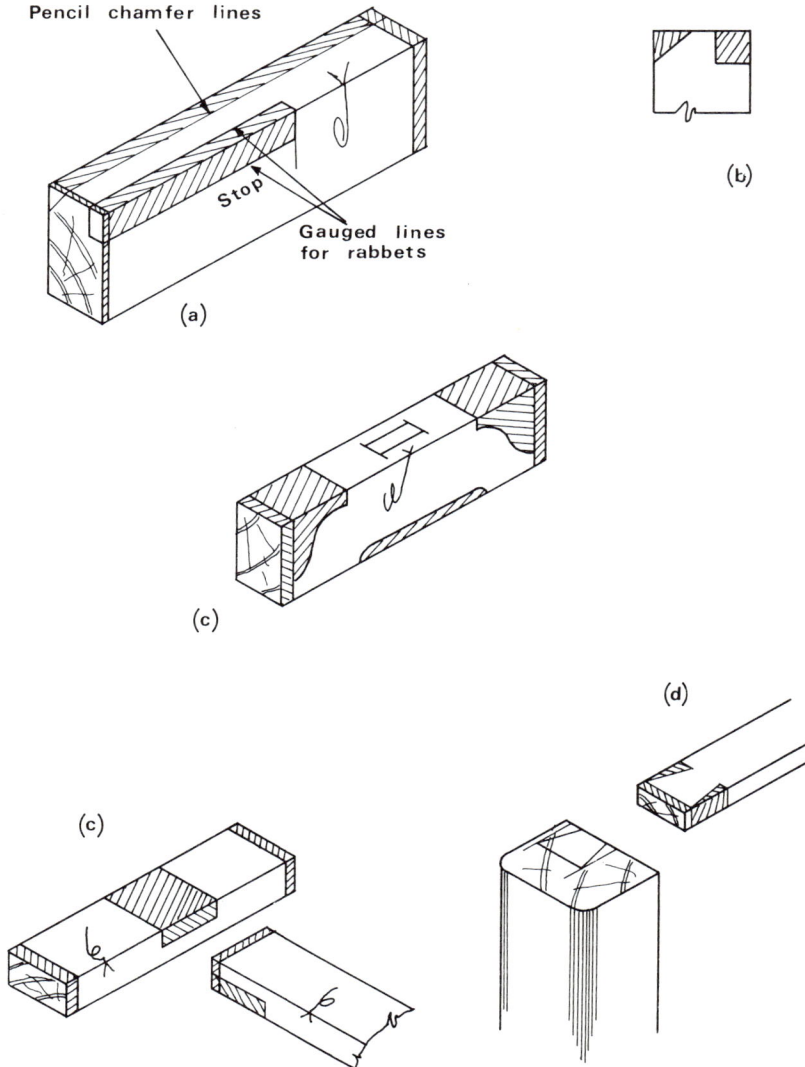

Pencil chamfer lines

Stop

Gauged lines for rabbets

(a)

(b)

(c)

(c)

(d)

Fig. 12.

a With wood-stocked try squares only the internal angle is made square.
b The calibrated steel square is 'square' both inside and outside.
c As far as possible always register square stock from face or face-edge of work piece.
d Rails are marked from the rod, thus

ensuring that they are all identical.
e Steel squares may be used inside the job. Wood-stocked squares may only be used from the outside.
f The mitre square is sometimes called the 'set 45'.
g Mitres are marked with the 'set 45' and checked with the square, for two 45° cuts should make 90°.

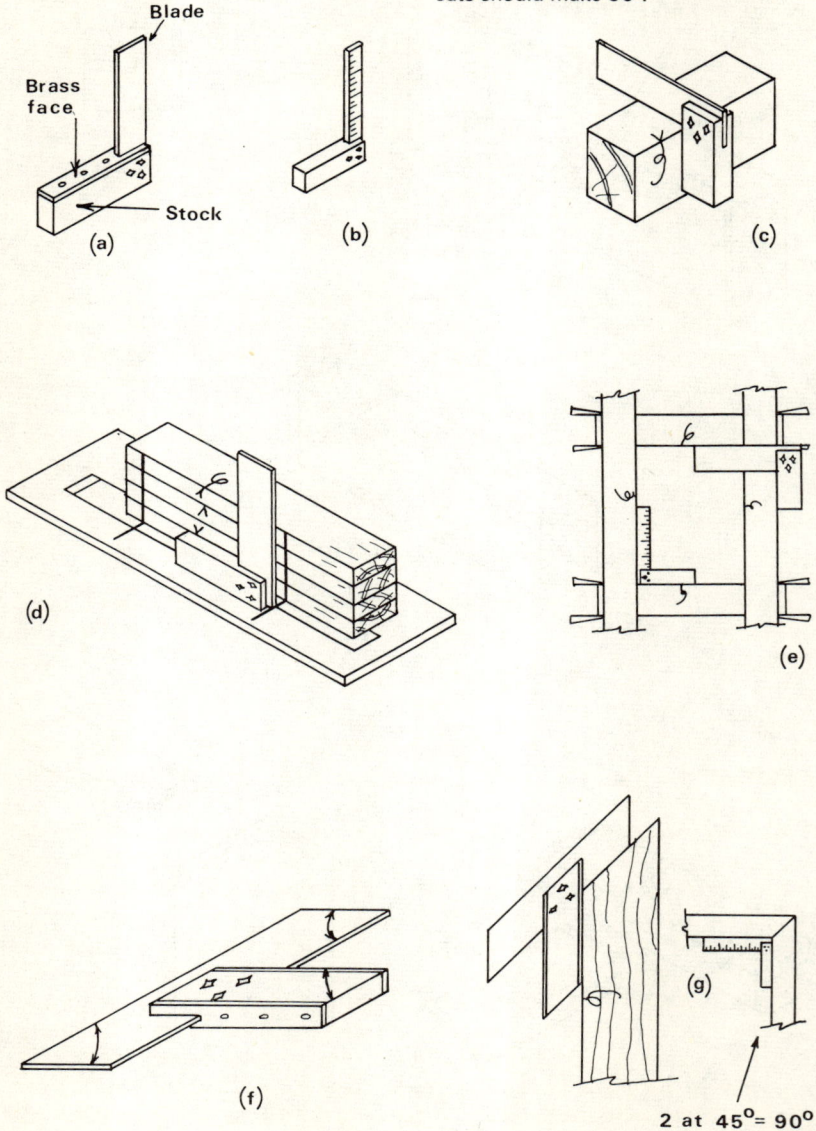

Blade

Brass
face

Stock

(a)

(b)

(c)

(d)

(e)

(f)

(g)

2 at 45° = 90°

stock. Unlike the old type wooden stock squares, these metal squares are intended for use from both edges of the stock and can be fitted into corners for such use. They vary in size from tiny pocket squares right up to 305 mm squares. The best for general home use is the one that has a blade of 150 mm.

The mitre square is so called because its blade is set at 45° to its stock, and this is the angle for common mitres for picture frames etc. It may be wood or metal stocked. The blade has its end at 45° to its sides. It may be used for setting sliding bevels to exact 45° angles.

Sliding Bevels

SLIDING BEVELS are used for transferring angles from drawings on to the wood, and for checking that angles being planed or sawn, are conforming to requirements. The sliding bevel has a slotted thin steel blade, which fits into a cast metal or wood, stock. With good quality wood stocked tools, the working faces may be faced with brass strip and the ends, brass pocketed.

The sliding blade will pivot through almost 360° and may be locked at any angle relative to the stock by a locking screw, which may be in the form of a short thumb lever, a counter-sunk cheese head screw, or, in metal bevels, by a long screw and wing nut that projects from the stock end.

If a bevel cut is indicated on the rod the 305 mm steel rule is placed close to, and parallel, to the face line of the job. The bevel stock is slid into contact with the firmly held rule, and the blade rotated until it sights accurately to the required bevel cut. The try square may be used to check this. The locking screw is then used to lock the blade.

Gauges

The two gauges required for general woodworking are the MARKING gauge, and the MORTISE gauge. To complete the kit another may be added, the CUTTING gauge.

These gauges are similar in appearance. Each has a stem, and a stock which slides along the stem, to be locked in any position by a thumbscrew or set-screw. The stock face may be faced with brass strip. At the working end of the stem there is a spur. It is the spur that varies the gauge. The marking gauge, used for marking fine precise lines that are later to be cut, has only one short needle pointed spur. The mortise gauge has two, with one adjustable relative to the other. By setting the points to the mortise chisel and then setting the stock to the correct distance from the inner point, twin lines may be gauged to indicate the correct position for cutting a mortise of the correct size. The gauge may be used also for marking for grooves. Many mortise gauges incorporate a third spur on the reverse side

Fig. 13.

a Marking gauges have one needle-pointed spur.
b Mortise gauges have two spurs, one of which is adjustable.
c Cutting gauges have a knife-edged spur.
d Cutting gauges may be used to scribe cross-grain lines before cutting.
e Rabbets are best marked with marking gauges.
f Mortise gauges give the guide lines necessary to guide the mortise chisel.
g Mortise gauge spurs must be set to the chisel that is to cut the mortise.

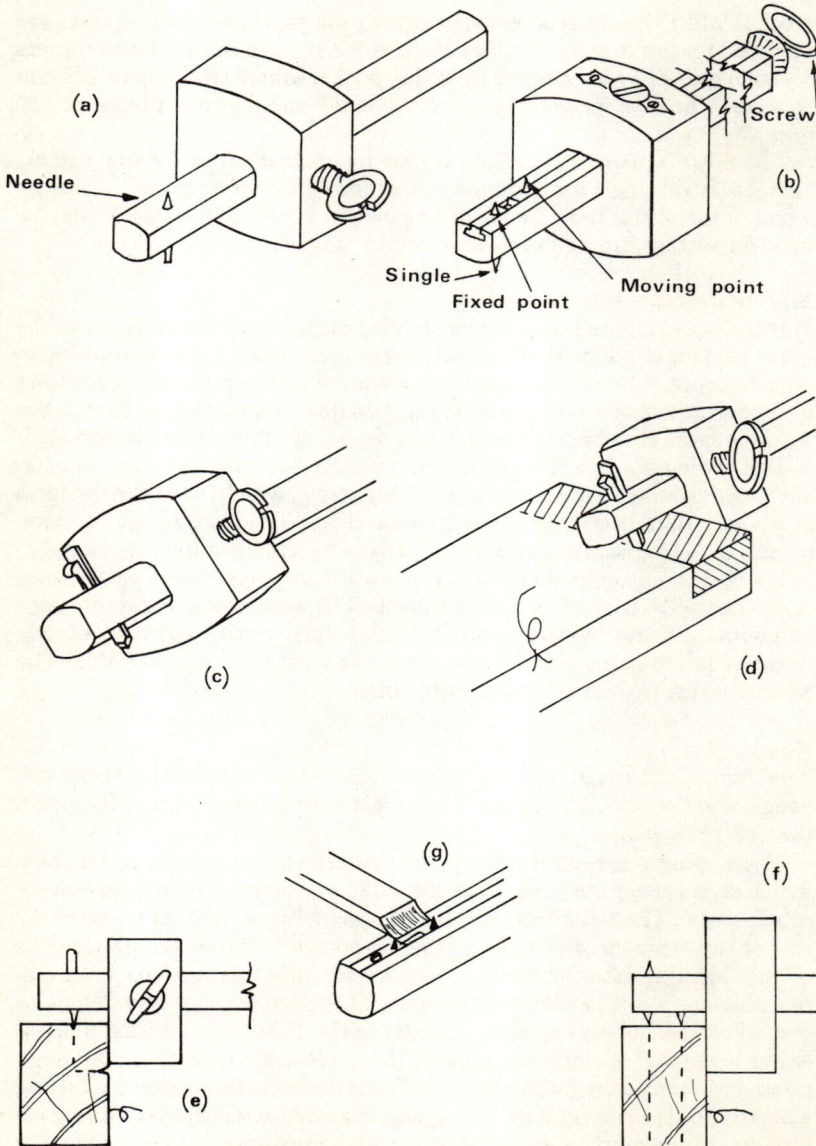

(a)

Needle →

(b)

Screw

Single →
Fixed point
Moving point

(c)

(d)

(g)

(f)

(e)

of the stem. This makes the tool into a combined mortise and marking gauge.

The third gauge is the cutting gauge, and this has a spur shaped to knife form. It is used for cutting. If a saw cut, or rebate is to be made across the grain close to the end of the wood, then the cutting gauge will cut the wood fibre cleanly to provide a guide for the saw or rabbet plane. Gauges are illustrated in Fig. 13.

Marking Knives and Dividers
Pencil points wear and may not be sufficiently accurate. Saws tend to give slightly whiskered cuts on the surface. Marking with a knife gives a precision position and avoids any whiskers after subsequent cuts. Marking knives may be permanent blades rivetted in wooden handles, but today, most are in the form of trimming knives, which means that they are useful for many other jobs of general cutting as well as that of marking out. Trimming knives have razor blade type blades in various shapes, all held into a cast metal handle.

Dividers are in compass form, with two legs, each sharp pointed. They may be friction grip, screw grip, or spring bow. The first has no other means of lock other than friction created by a pre-set screw. Screw grips have one leg connected to the other by a quadrant, which may be locked by screws to maintain leg position. The spring bow has the legs permanently sprung open until they are closed by the action of an adjustment screw.

Dividers are for transferring measurements, and are useful too for scribing. To mark out a mortise that is to be repeated several times along a stile, it is safer to set divider points than it is to rely on the rule and pencil. Fig. 14 shows the use of marking knife and dividers.

BASIC GEOMETRY
Geometry is concerned with distance—or measurement, and its relationship to fixed and moveable points. And this is really what marking out is all about—the position and shape of one line related to another. If we think of a line as being the path of a travelling point and we think of the travelling point as always having a special relationship with another point or line, we should begin to have an understanding of geometry. We can then think of a circle as being a flat or 'plane' figure whose boundary is always at a constant distance from a central point, and we begin to understand the peculiar language with which geometry is defined. If we then think of a square as being a flat (or plane) figure whose sides are all of equal length, and whose four angles are all equal, we can see that if a square is rotated (like a flag) about one side, it will generate, in the air, a cylinder.

Fig. 14.
a and b Metal-handled general purpose
knife and wood-handled marking knife.
c, d and e Friction grip dividers, screw
grip dividers, and spring-bow dividers.
f, g, h and i Dividers are used for
measuring, marking out, and scribing
where one part must fit another.

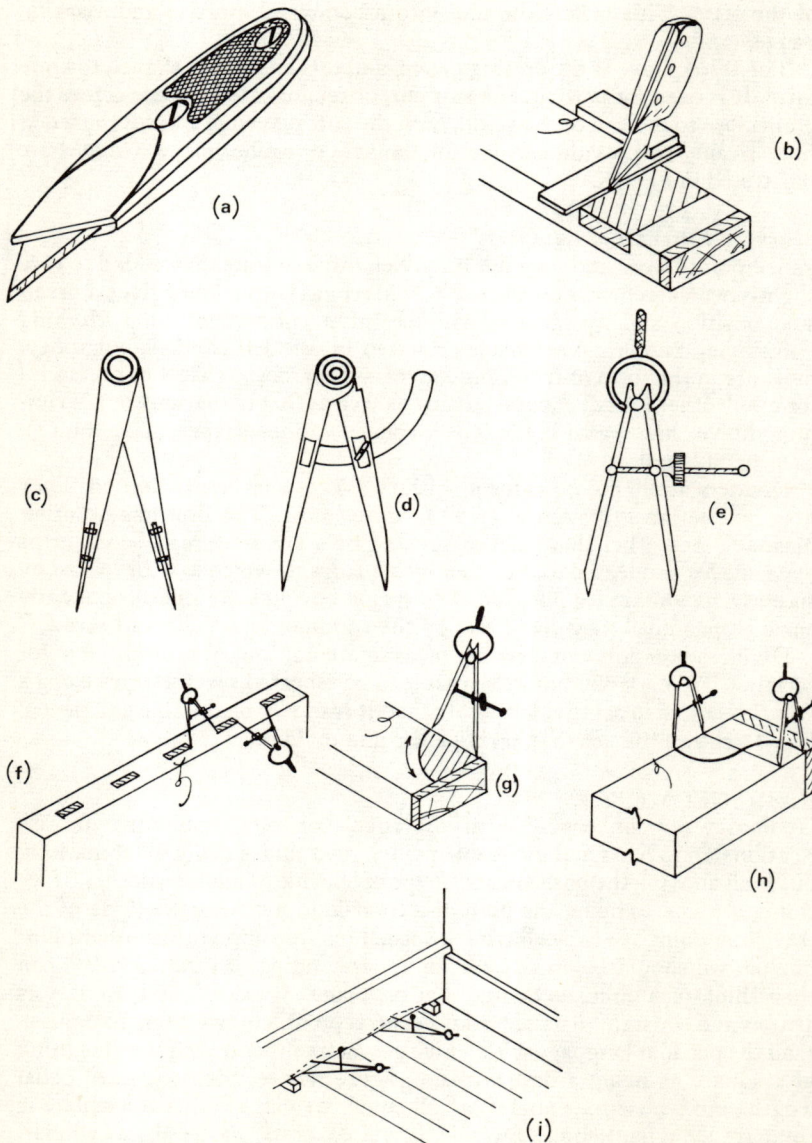

(a)

(b)

(c)

(d)

(e)

(f)

(g)

(h)

(i)

Both top and bottom of the cylinder will be identical circles, and its height will be equal to the length of side of the square.

The home woodworker is not often called upon to understand much geometry, but he must be able to use basic geometry to check for squareness and to mark out shapes. Putting a roof on a lean-to enclosure, or even to a dog kennel, calls for this basic geometrical know-how.

5 Jointing the Case

JOINTS AND JOINT STRENGTH

Before marking and cutting a joint the question must be asked, and answered—'What am I trying to achieve, and what is the purpose of the joint?' This is necessary because different jobs require different construction methods. A simple packing case for a one-off job certainly does not require the precise and elaborate secret and mitred dovetail joint of the decorative jewellery casket. Neither does the dog kennel require the framed mortise and tenon door of the house.

BASIC PRINCIPLES

For many years people have been endeavouring to lay down a list of simple basic rules. Some of these suggestions have been adapted, some have not, but to generalise, joint construction must fulfil the following requirements: the finished joint must have had as little material removed as possible, leaving maximum strength in each section, and providing adequate grip for any mechanical fastenings (nails, screws etc.). Where a load has to be carried, it must be carried as far as is possible, at right angles (perpendicular) to its support. (A door-frame head should sit on the jambs and not be tenoned into it).

Any extra strength additions (screws, nails, plates etc.) must not be so large as to weaken the wood, nor so small as to pull through, or out when load is applied.

Cutting design should have joint faces as large as possible to give maximum glueing area and to spread the applied load. This requirement must be considered together with the previous requirement to cut away minimum timber.

Finally, timber itself must be considered. In Chapter One it was shown that as timber dries it shrinks and moves. Joint design must allow for this.

Adding all of these requirements together we can safely say that simple joints are more likely to be efficient than complicated ones because of the element of woodworker skill.

Fig. 15 illustrates some of the above principles.

JOINT DESIGN

The main functions of joints are to lengthen, widen, or join wood sections. The home woodworker does not often have the need to lengthen timber, but sometimes this may be necessary for, perhaps, a ridge piece for a garage or shed. The simplest form of lengthening joint is the plain SCARF, where ends are tapered then glued and screwed. A reasonably accurate saw cut would do, although a planed surface is better. To improve the scarf and to give some degree of mechanical strength, a key is added. Stronger again

Fig. 15.

a Stubbed tenons between jambs and the head will prevent water penetration, and external diagonal braces will give rigidity.

b Where corners are to be seen, mitred joints will give a better appearance than haunched mortise and tenon joints.

c Tongued joints must be long grained.

Tongues in cross-grain, or in chip board, easily shear.

d Thin tenons will give easily at the shoulder.

e Tenons that are thick or that are mortised too close to the end of the stile will split the stile.

f Maximum thickness at all joints is (continued on following page)

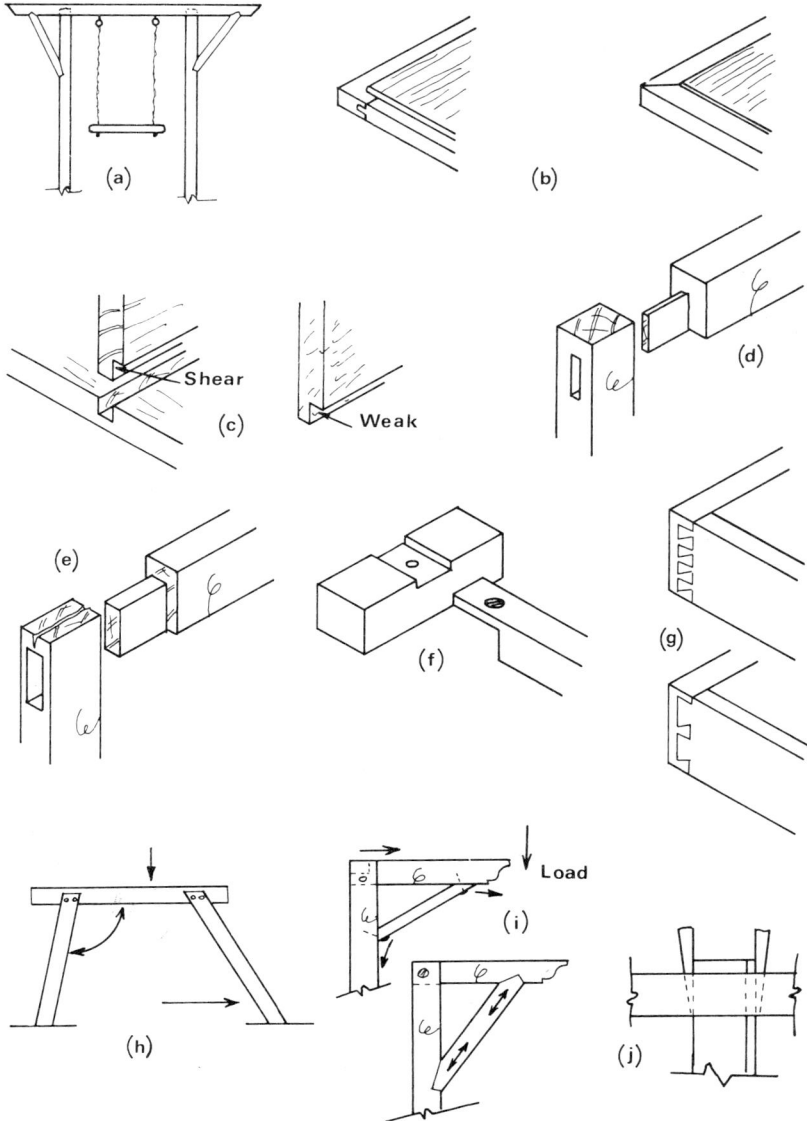

(a)

(b)

(c) Shear

Weak

(d)

(e)

(f)

(g)

(h)

Load

(i)

(j)

required to prevent shearing and splitting.

g Machine dovetails are regular in appearance. When hand cut the tails are made wider and the pins made as fine as possible.

h For load carrying, legs must be as near to upright as will give sufficient stability.

If leg spread is too great the load will tend to spread them even further.

i Struts should abut with a shoulder cut square to the run of the strut. Struts should be as near vertical as is reasonable.

j Wide tenons shrink and this allows wedges to fall out.

is the lapped scarf where two shoulders are added for abutment. The addition of folding wedges makes the joint easy to assemble and more rigid.

Widening

For solid wood the easiest joint is the RUBBED or BUTT joint, which is sufficiently strong for most work. The two edges are planed straight and square until they fit. Most modern adhesives require cramping, so instead of rubbing the joint until the glue penetrates and begins to hold, cramps must be used. This requires that the boards to be jointed are reasonably flat. Perhaps the more efficient in strength and assembly for home woodworkers, is the LOOSE TONGUE joint, where both edges are planed straight, and then a groove is ploughed, into which is fitted a plywood tongue. This assists in keeping the board surfaces flush. An easier and cheaper form of butt joint is achieved if CORRUGATED FASTENERS are driven in, but this spoils surface appearance. Solid tongues are not so easy to cut and are not of much importance. DOWELLED joints are strong but require fairly accurate boring. SECRET screwing still has a part to play if the work is to be taken apart later on, and is not to be glued, or if no cramps are available.

Widening of other materials, such as plywood, chipboard and blockwood is mostly done with loose tongues, although for chipboard, the tongues must be fairly thin and used only as keys. There is very little strength in edge-on chipboard.

Carcase and Construction Joints

There are so many of these joints that a formal description of each serves little purpose. Fig. 16 shows a range of corner joints. Fig. 17 shows a further range of corner joints and Figs. 18 and 19 show applications of various special joints.

SIMPLE MECHANICS

The object of most jobs is to make them rigid. The achievement of this is only possible if the job has been designed with load-bearing in mind. Quite simply this means that the house walls must be able to carry their own weight, the weight of the floors, the weight of the roof, and any extra loading applied by wind, snow and rain. A shelf must be able to carry the weight of goods stacked on it without collapsing or bowing.

At project design stage, loads and forces must be considered. Modern production dining chairs have slender legs, quite capable of supporting the applied load, yet furniture of earlier periods often had very large and clumsy legs. The homeworker always tends to make sections too large—'to be

58

Fig. 16.

a 'Stopped' housings will improve the appearance of the front of the job.
b Where housing is used close to an end it is 'shouldered'. This gives extra strength.
c Horizontal shelves tend to pull out of housings. An improvement is to make dovetail housings.
d Chipboard corners may be dowelled.
e Alternative corner joint for chipboard, plywood or blockboard.
f A solid wood corner may be used to give a better appearance where man-made boards are used.

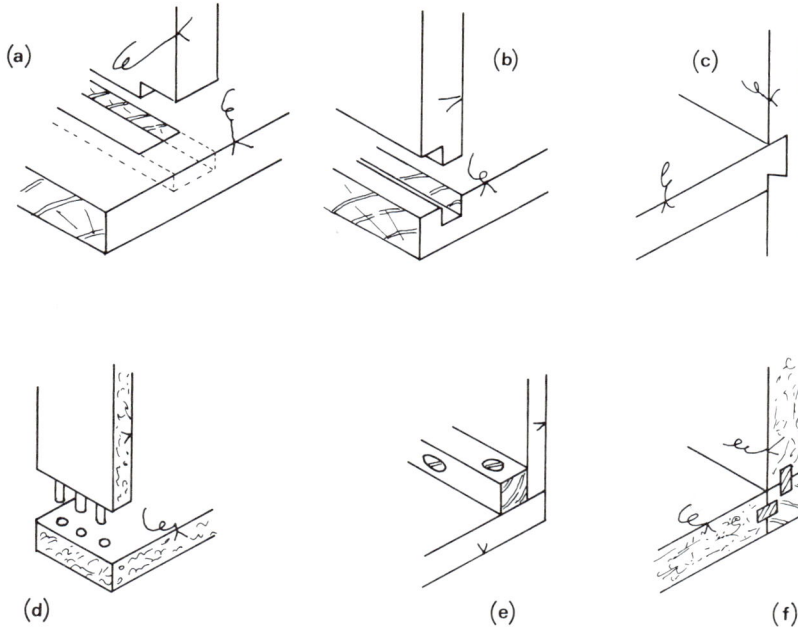

on the safe side'. A square section that is to carry a direct downwards load must be large enough in cross-sectional area to be 'stiff' under load. A square section pinned and glued to stiff plywood will carry such a load even if only a fraction of the cross-sectional area of the first square section. Material 50 mm × 50 mm is stronger in compression and stiffer in flexion than material 25 mm × 100 mm (1 in. × 4 in.) although both have the same cross-sectional area.

The mechanics of buildings are complex. We need only to know a few basic principles.

Mechanics Applied to Woodwork

The triangle is the only rigid frame, and if we understand this we should know enough to manage. All squared frames subject to load must be triangulated. All supports to loads must be triangulated. Light box carcases must be triangulated.

Fig. 20 explains this insistence on triangulation and gives examples of applications.

Fig. 17.
a Tongued and mitred corners.
b Corner held with 'Knock-Down' fittings.
c Tongued and grooved corner.
d Rabbeted and blocked corner.
e Plain mitre with 'feather' keys.
f Dovetail angles should be between 1 in 6 and 1 in 8.
g Solidwood or plywood sides may be lap-dovetailed to solid front. Chipboard may be dowelled. Plywood may be 'slip' dovetailed.

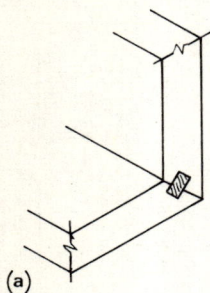

(a)

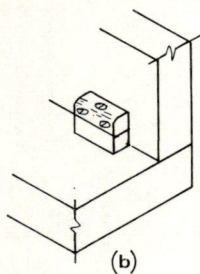

(b)

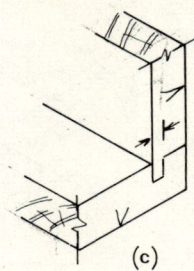

(c)

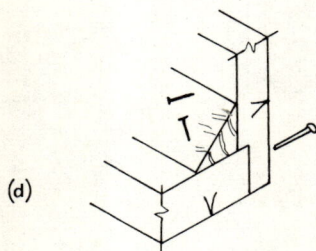

(d)

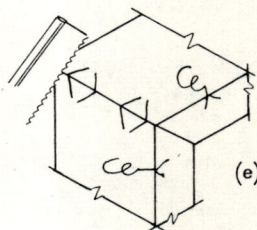

(e)

1 in 6
or
1 in 8

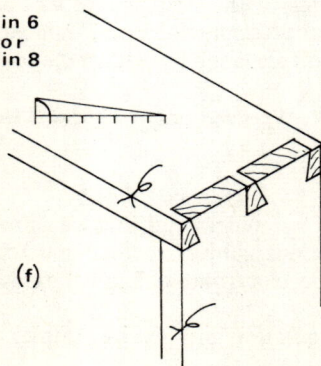

(f)

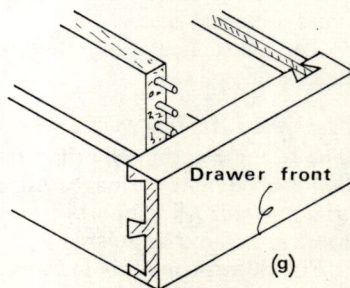

Drawer front

(g)

Fig. 18.

a Joint arrangement for two-panel door.
b Tenons are haunched back to prevent stile ends from splitting.
c Tenons should be no more than one-third of rail thickness.
d Wide rails have tenons divided into two to minimise the effects of shrinkage.
e Tenons should be no more than five times the thickness, or three-fifths of the rail width.

f Tenons: Haunched, Wedged, Pinned and Foxed.
g Side dovetailed tenons will carry tensile load.
h Plug tenons are much stronger than housings for wide boards.
i Pegged bridle joint.
j Twin-double tenons will allow space for mortise lock.
k Traditional 'Tusk Tenon' used in floors between trimmers and trimming joists.

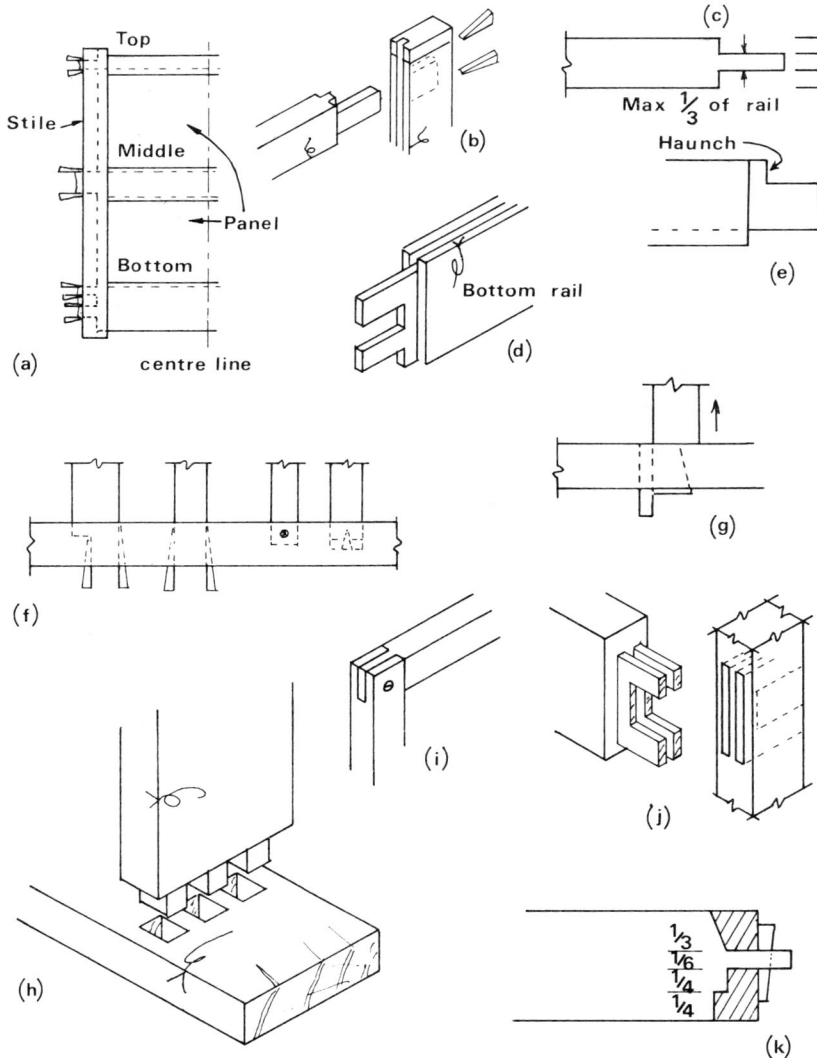

Fig. 19.
a Tee halving; Dovetail halving; Notching; Cogging.
b Table with drawer; corner construction.
c Cross-halving.
d Rabbeted work requires long and short shoulders on tenons.

e Moulded sash stuff must be short scribed. Part 'X' on the stile fits into part 'X' on rail. The franking, 'Y' on the rail fits into 'Y' on stile.
f Mouldings may be mitred if scribing appears to be too difficult.

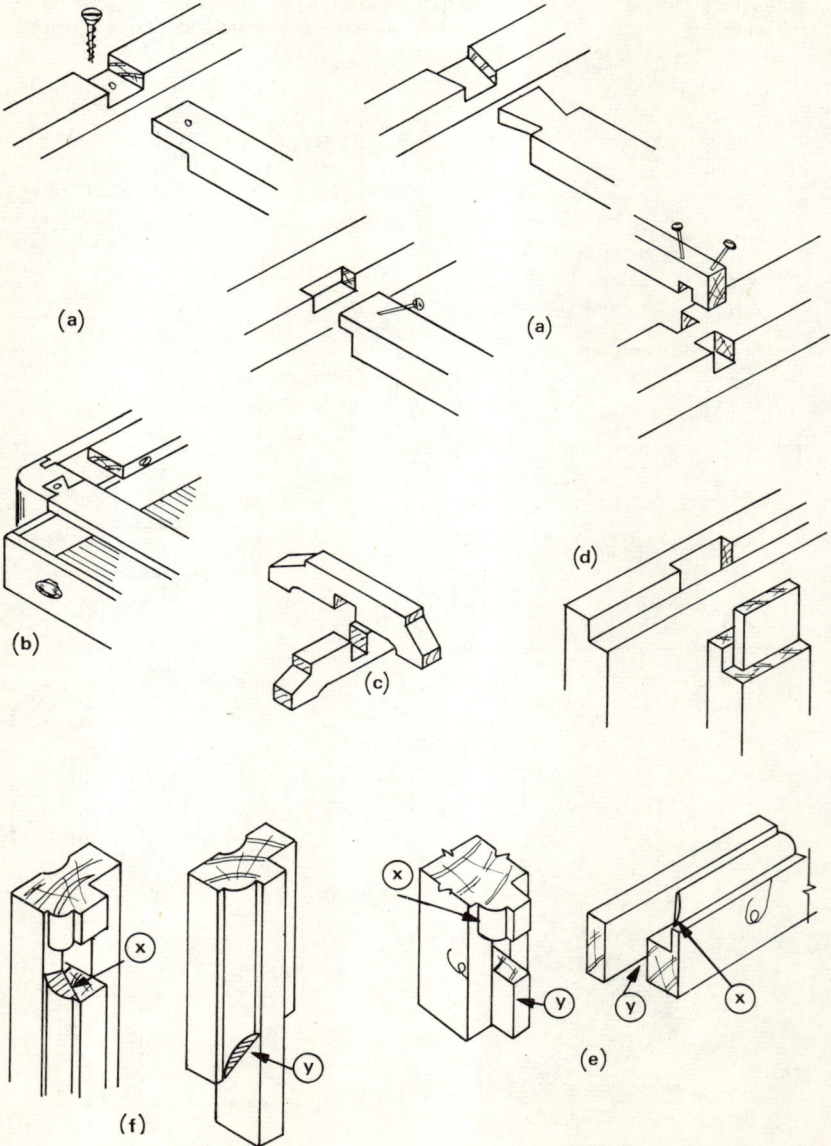

(a)

(a)

(b)

(c)

(d)

(e)

(f)

Fig. 20.

a With rigid joints no load will distort or deflect these triangles.

b Diagonal strutting stiffens floor joists.

c The horizontal collar triangulates simple roof framing.

d A traditional porch uses struts to carry weight and these must be substantial.

e A match-boarded, ledged and braced door relies on triangulation to maintain its shape.

f A wire rod may be used as a 'tie' to support a load for it is in tension, not compression.

g Brace 'x' gives no support for it is tension. Brace 'y' gives full support for it is compression.

h Either brace/strut 'x' or tie 'y' will keep posts upright to oppose pull of wire strainers.

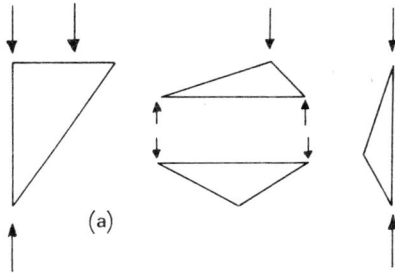

(a)

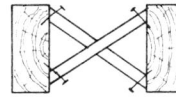

(b)

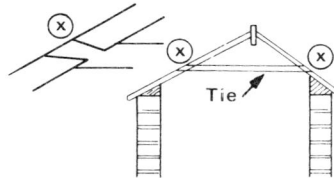

Tie

(c)

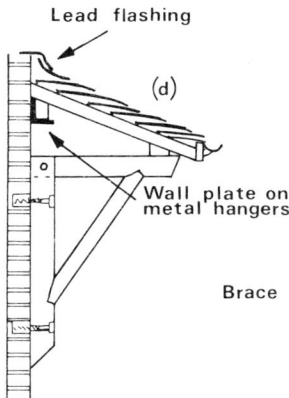

Lead flashing

(d)

Wall plate on metal hangers

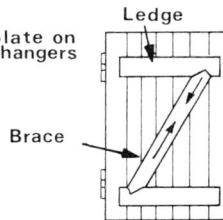

Ledge

Brace

(e)

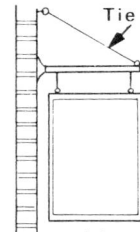

Tie

(f)

(g) Load

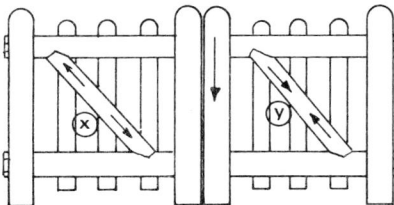

Strainer

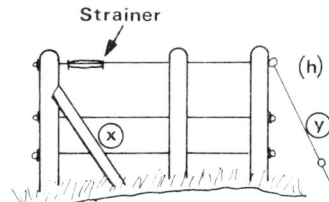

(h)

TOOLS USED. CUTTING METHODS

Saws, planes, chisels, bits, and, in fact, all tools with sharp edges are used for joint cutting. Saws and planes have previously been explained, for both have a fairly complex technology. The remaining tools are straightforward.

Chisels, of three types, are simple forged steel bars, ground at one end to a sharp edge, and having a TANG at the other end which is driven into the turned wood or moulded plastic handle. A brass FERRULE surrounds the handle and chisel tang to prevent splitting.

The three types of chisel are: the FIRMER, the BEVELLED EDGE and the MORTISE.

The firmer has a flat, square-edged blade and is the 'Jack of all Trades Tool'. It is made as narrow as 3 mm ($\frac{1}{8}$ in.) or as wide as 50 mm (2 in.).

The bevelled edge chisel is of lighter cross-section, and has its long edges bevelled. This gives it greater facility for handling into small joints, and makes PARING easier, Paring means slicing rather than chopping. In size the bevelled edge runs from 3 mm to 50 mm ($\frac{1}{8}$ in. to 2 in.).

The mortise chisel is longer and more heavy in section. It has a square section blade and is made in two styles. The lighter version is called a SASH·MORTISE.

All quality chisels have the tang end forged with a shock shoulder which abuts the end of the handle. The heavier mortise chisels have also a leather washer between the shoulder and the end of the handle. This takes the drive force when the end of the handle is struck with the MALLET.

The mallet is the wooden striking tool used for driving all chisels. It, the mallet, has MASS (bulk) and when swung, gathers MOMENTUM. The energy build up in the mallet head is expended into the chisel in the form of drive force on impact.

The mortise chisel (both versions) is made from 3mm to 18 mm ($\frac{1}{8}$ in. to $\frac{3}{4}$ in.). Chisels and a mallet are shown in Fig. 21.

HOLE BORING

A quick way to remove wood is to bore it away. Many types of drills and bits are available but for home use the most common are JENNINGS, MORSE DRILLS and the SLICK BIT. The first of these, the jennings, is a TWIST BIT. There are several types of twist bits, but the only difference lies in the formation of the cutting end. All have a centre point, screw threaded or brad (square), and all have two cutting teeth. Only the jennings has, in addition, two spur or wing cutters that cut a scribed line as they rotate; this gives a clean entry.

Twist bits are used in a HAND·BRACE and must have a square tapered, forged shank. Their stems are round, and the body of the bit has two long

Fig. 21.
The standard range of chisels is shown at
the page top. At centre are a mallet, and
both firmer and scribing gouges. The
lower drawing shows the use of a mortise lock chisel.

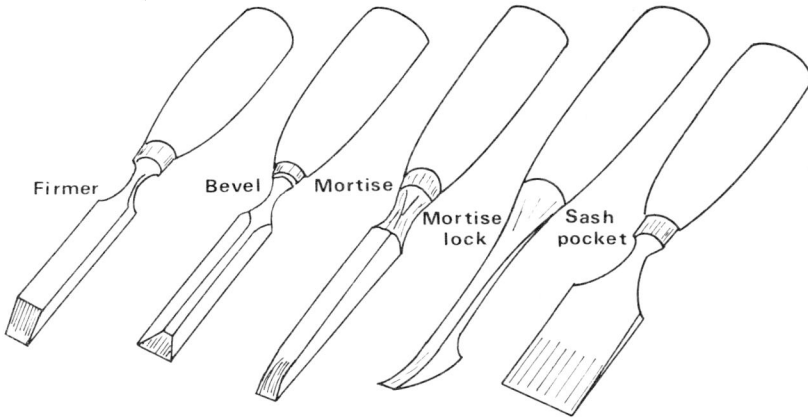

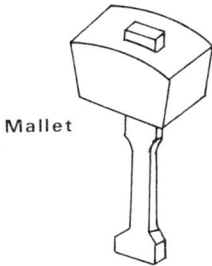

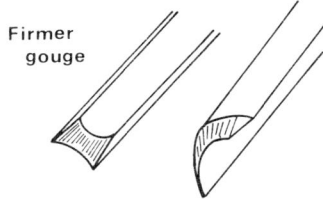

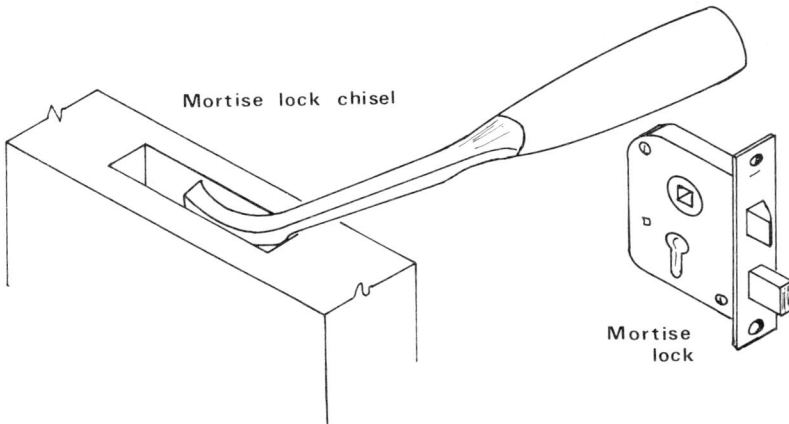

Firmer   Bevel   Mortise

Mortise   Sash
lock   pocket

Mallet   Firmer   Scribing
gouge   gouge

Mortise lock chisel

Mortise
lock

helical flutes ground, to carry away chips from the hole. The screw thread assists in pulling the bit into the wood. Twist bits run in size from 4 mm to 35 mm ($\frac{3}{16}$ in. to $1\frac{1}{2}$ in.).

Morse drills are sometimes called JOBBERS STRAIGHT SHANK DRILLS. They are shorter, and have round, parallel shranks. Their cutting ends are ground to a flat point, and are used either in a WHEEL·BRACE or an electric drill. They are useful for pre-boring for screws.

The SLICK·BIT is a patent type of electric drill bit. It has a plain round shank to fit on to the drill chuck, and this is used for all size cuts. The cutting end is flat steel blank ground with two leading cutting edges that terminate into scribing spurs. They have a brad point centre. They are sold as a set, and in size will bore holes from 6 mm to 32 mm ($\frac{1}{4}$ to $1\frac{1}{4}$ in.).

Other bits or drills that are useful are the CENTRE bit, the EXPANDING bit, and the FORSTNER bit. The centre bit has a screw centre point, one cutting edge and one scribing edge. Such bits are intended for shallow holes, and range in size from 44 mm to 56 mm ($\frac{3}{16}$ in. to $2\frac{1}{4}$ in.). They are used in the hand-brace. The expanding bit is extremely useful for jobbing carpentry, for they are adjustable bits, and the user selects each setting. They have a screw centre, a spur cutter, and two clearance cutters, one of which is adjustable with the spur. To give a complete range in sizes, two expanding bits are required. The smaller cuts from 12 mm to 35 mm, and the larger from 20 mm to 75 mm ($\frac{1}{2}$ in. to 3 in. in all). The forstner bits are special bits for use either for cutting holes to be plugged or for rapid clearance away of material in large housings. Their design allows them to be used for overlapping holes. They have a broad centre, two cutters, and two almost semi-circular scribing wings. It is these wings that, running in the scribe they have made, prevent any side drift of the bit. Thus overlapping holes become possible.

The Hand Brace

This is the heavy duty boring tool. Fitted with the correct bit, large and deep holes are quickly made. They consist of a cranked main piece, a rotating hand grip, a chuck, and a breast pad (rotating). They are sold by size of sweep, which is the total diameter swing of centre handle. The best version has a ratchet chuck, which allows rotation in enclosed places.

The wheel brace has a mechanical method of turning for the bit. They are only of use for round shank bits and those of smaller size. They are best used for screw pre-boring and for COUNTER SINKING. They have two handles, one in-line with bit, and one at right angles to the bit. There is a handwheel which, when rotated, drives a spur gear that in turn drives a smaller gear. Thus the chuck is rotated.

USE OF CHISELS AND BITS

Cutting mortises becomes routine if tackled in the correct way. The guide rules are simple. The mortise is always marked out with the mortise gauge set to the width of the chisel chosen. Mortises that go right through, called THROUGH MORTISES, must be cut from both sides. Chisels and bits must be held truly perpendicular and not allowed to wander from side to side. A sight-line on the bench is useful here. Chisels should never be allowed to lever on the mortise ends; this spoils the look and fit. There must always be something solid and heavy below the workpiece. It nearly always pays to cut the mortise first before the tenon, for tenons are more easily adjusted, although the aim should be 'First-Time-Fit.'

CHOPPING THE MORTISE

Firmly cramp job to bench. Stand in-line with run of rail or stile. Place chisel in centre of mortise with bevel facing away. Strike with mallet. Move back, cut once more. Repeat this until chisel is within 1−2 mm ($\frac{1}{16}$ in.) from mortise end. Start again in centre and repeat. Then reverse chisel and work back to other end of mortise. The chisel bevel will cause opening slot to be deeper towards the ends.

Now chop more deeply until about half-way through. Reverse wood top to bottom and repeat cutting operations. Chisel should break through. Knock out debris or push through with short lath and mallet. Use chisel now with bevel facing away and with its edge set about 0·5 mm ($\frac{1}{32}$ in.) from line. Chop vertically downwards and note that chisel bevel has driven chisel face back to the correct margin line. Repeat for other three margin lines. Clean out.

For larger mortises than those conveniently chopped out, use a correct size jennings bit and bore as many holes along mortise as possible. Chop out remainder. For even larger mortises, use the forstner bit. This will allow almost complete removal of waste wood. When boring right through, work from one side until screw point breaks through. Then reverse wood and use break through point as centre for finishing the hole.

CUTTING TENONS

Mark clearly with gauge set as it was for marking mortises. As the chisel went inside the mortise lines, so the tenon saw must go outside. In this way, with accurate cutting, the maximum error possible will be the double width of the gauge line, which is almost beyond measurement.

Place work end-up in vice but angled at about 45° away. Cut from top corner, sighting along both the line on the side of the work and the line on the end. Cut until the shoulder line is reached. Cut other face of tenon but to the other side of the line. Reverse work and repeat. Now position work vertically in vice. Use saw horizontal and allow it to follow into cuts already made. If the rail is to be made shaped in section (stuck) then this is now done before the tenon cheeks are removed.

Hold rail (or workpiece) tightly up against the end stop of the bench hook and using thumb as guide, saw carefully across shoulder line. Turn work over and repeat. Tenon should now fit. If not, use a bullnose plane very lightly, checking as you go.

Fig. 22 illustrates these techniques.

HOUSING AND HALF-LAPS

Housings are first sawn down, using a bench hook and tenon saw. Then, using correct width chisel, the waste is removed working from both edges of wood. Halving joints are cut from both edge, and the waste may be pared away rather than chopped if the grain is wild (curly).

Stopped housings are first bored at the inner end using a forstner bit. Then the margin lines are sawn, and the waste chiselled out. If a suitable forstner bit is not available a short mortise is chopped at the inner end of the housing; this permits the saw cut to be carried right through to inner end of housing.

Finally, for through housing, stopped housings, or half-laps, a ROUTER is used to level the bottom. Routers are basically a flat sole plate, a hooked and very low angle cutter, and two hand-holds.

Fig. 23 shows these methods.

DOVETAIL JOINTS

Dovetail joints interlock. They resist tensional pull along the line of the wood member carrying the tails. Thus for a case joint, the vertical sides would have the tails cut and the horizontal sides, the sockets. The sockets receive the tails. Wood shears easily along the grain so the angle of the tail side is critical. Too great an angle and the tail corners shear away easily. Too low an angle and the wedging action of the tails will split the sockets when loading is applied.

Dovetail joints are mainly used for box-like constructions, although they are sometimes used for strengthening housings and half-laps. Here we are concerned with the box-like applications. There are four of these joints. The plain BOX dovetail, the LAP dovetail, the SECRET·LAP dovetail, and the SECRET MITRE DOVETAIL. The last two are exceptionally difficult to cut and fit, and require a high degree of skill and know-how. Both the secret-lap and the secret-mitre have sockets and tails concealed. With the mitred version the joint looks as if it is a straight mitre, whereas the secret-lap looks as if the joint has been simply lapped together and glued. Fig. 24 il-

Fig. 22.
The stages in cutting and fitting of tenons
are shown from 1 to 7. Either a panel saw
or back saw may be used for the cheek
cuts. Tenon saw and bench hook are
used to cut shoulders, and the bullnose
and shoulder planes are used to fit tenon.
To bore through with the jennings bit, it is
used from both faces of wood.

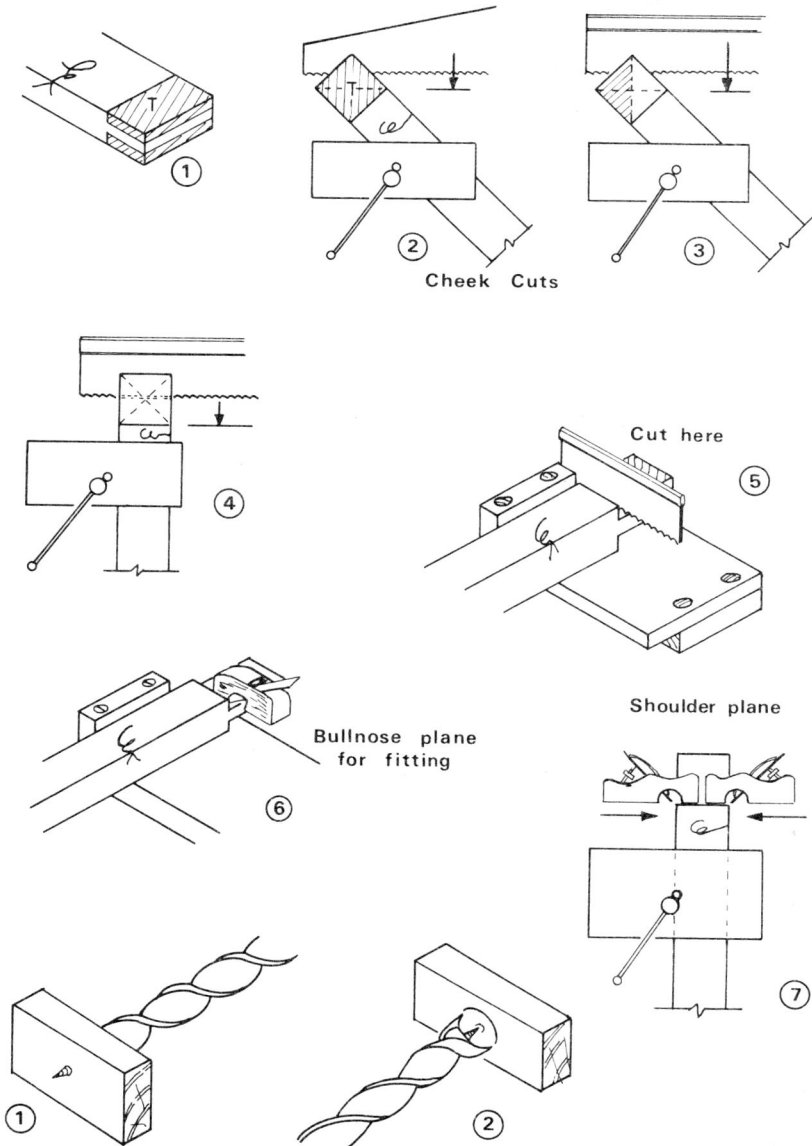

Cheek Cuts

Cut here

Bullnose plane
for fitting

Shoulder plane

Fig. 23.
The stages of cutting through housings
are shown here from 1 to 4 and from 5 to
7 for stopped housings.

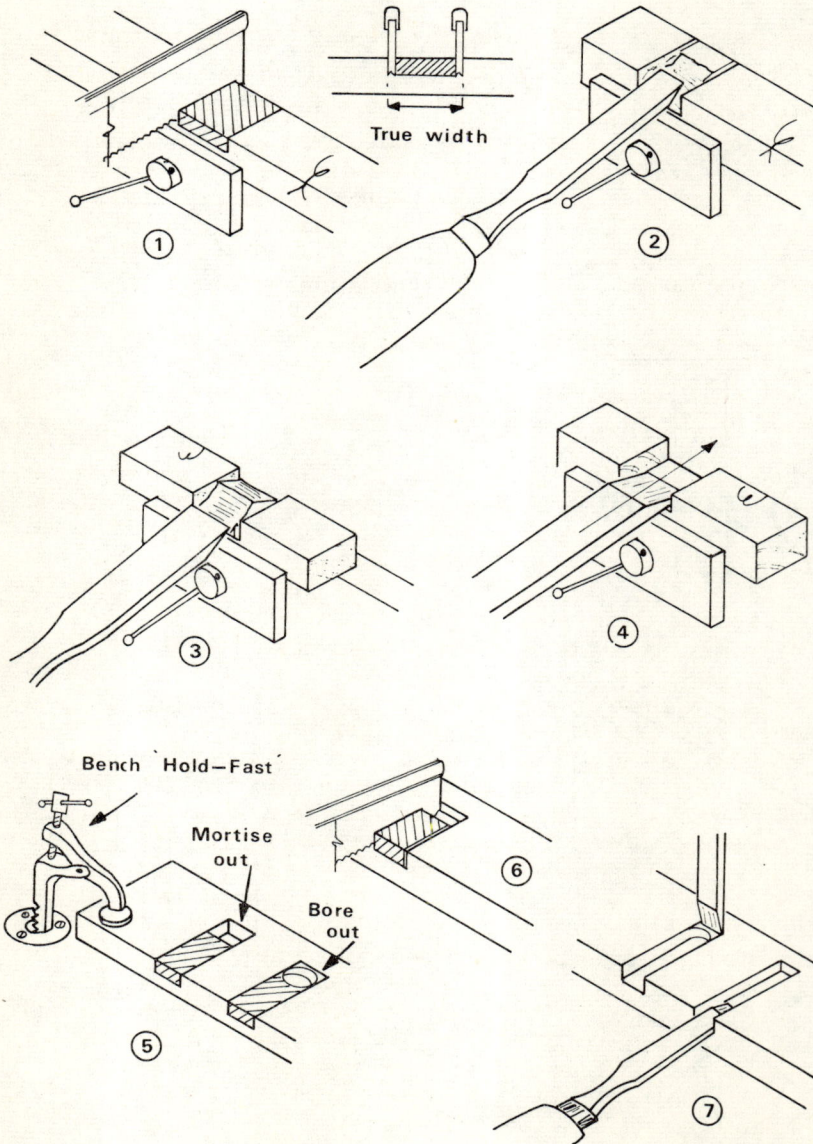

True width

① ②

③ ④

Bench Hold—Fast

Mortise
out

Bore
out

⑥

⑤ ⑦

lustrates the four dovetail joints, and shows the method of starting to cut joints.

BOX DOVETAILS

The joint must be thought out bearing in mind: the direction of load, appearance, and the placing of tails relative to grooves or rebates in the job.

When these points have been decided, the relative widths of sockets to tail spacing must be considered. For coarse work such as softwood tool boxes etc. fairly wide tails may be used, say three across a box 125 mm (5 in.) deep, with due allowance made for lid position. For fine, hand-made hardwood jobs, feather dovetails are used (for improved appearance) where the tails are relatively broad but the wood left between them is almost non-existent.

When the size and position have been decided on (sketching on paper will help) the ends of wood are cut and planed very accurately square. A cutting gauge is set to the wood thickness and fine lines are gauged all round all the ends of the pieces of wood. The gauge is used with the thumb behind the cutter in the stem, the forefinger wrapped round the stock, and the other three fingers gripping the stem. This is known as the 'Thumb, One, Three' grip. It applies to nearly all woodworking tools: the saw, the plane, the square, the gauge, the screwdriver and so on. For gauging, the wood is rested on the bench and the gauge is firmly pushed away—always away, to keep stock, stem and cutter always in correct contact.

The tails are now marked in pencil on the two short box ends. Then the tail ends are marked across with the square. Both of the box ends may be marked and cut as one piece if they are pinned together. A sliding bevel is set for the 1 in 6, or 1 in 7 angle, and the tail sides are marked.

The two pieces, still pinned, are gripped in the vice and sawcuts are made down the tail sides to the gauged line. See Fig. 24.

One of the box sides is now placed in the bench vice, face side in, and with its tail end above the vice cheeks. The two box ends are now placed down on to the projecting end of the side in the vice and a piece of wood is used to raise them level. They are firmly held by hand pressure and the saw is dropped through each saw cut in turn until it clearly marks the end of the box side below.

Mark the saw cut marks down vertically with a try-square. Shade in waste, then run the saw down to the gauge marks around the box side. The saw must keep to the waste side of the previously made saw cut mark.

Chopping Out

If the gaps between the tails are reasonably large, and also if the sockets are

Fig. 24.
a Box or lapped dovetail.
b Secret lap dovetail.
c Pin two box ends together and cut to waste side of lines.
d Use saw cuts as guides to mark sockets from tails. Cut to waste sides of lines.

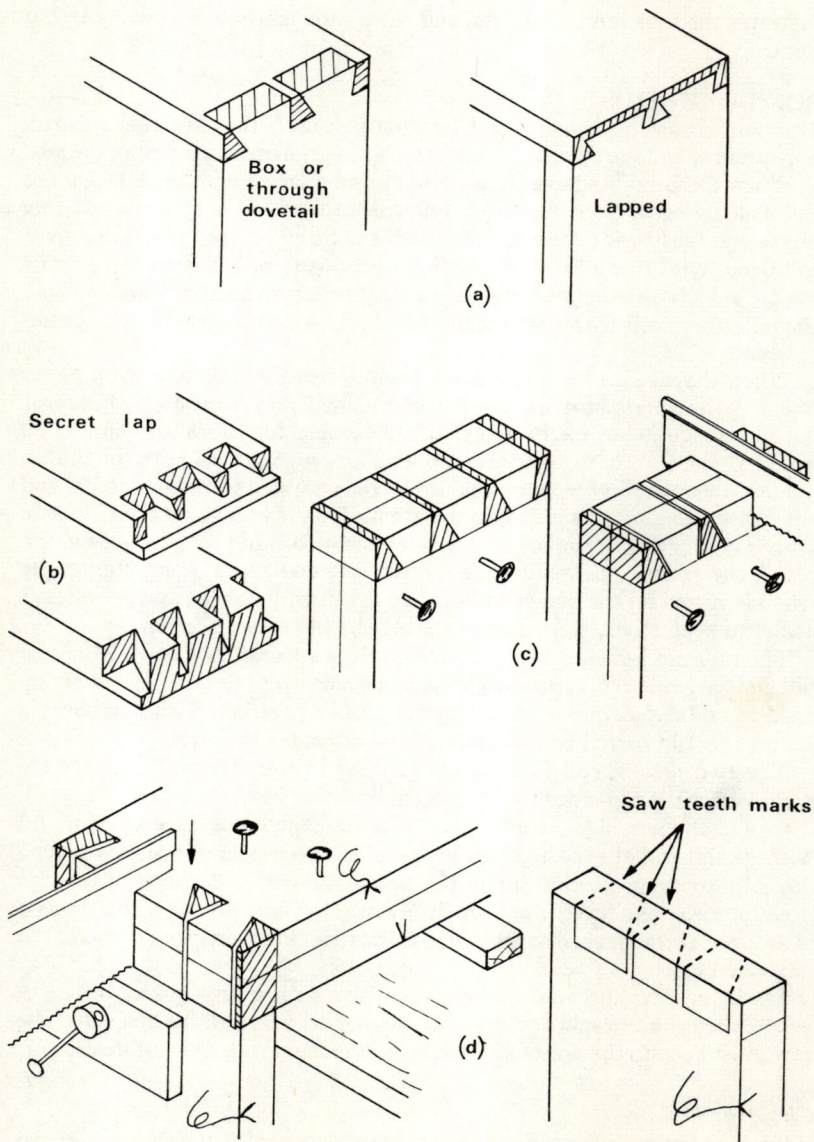

Box or through dovetail

Lapped

(a)

Secret lap

(b)

(c)

Saw teeth marks

(d)

72

Fig. 25.
a The coping saw may be used to
remove bulk of waste.
b Chisels are then used to complete the
work.

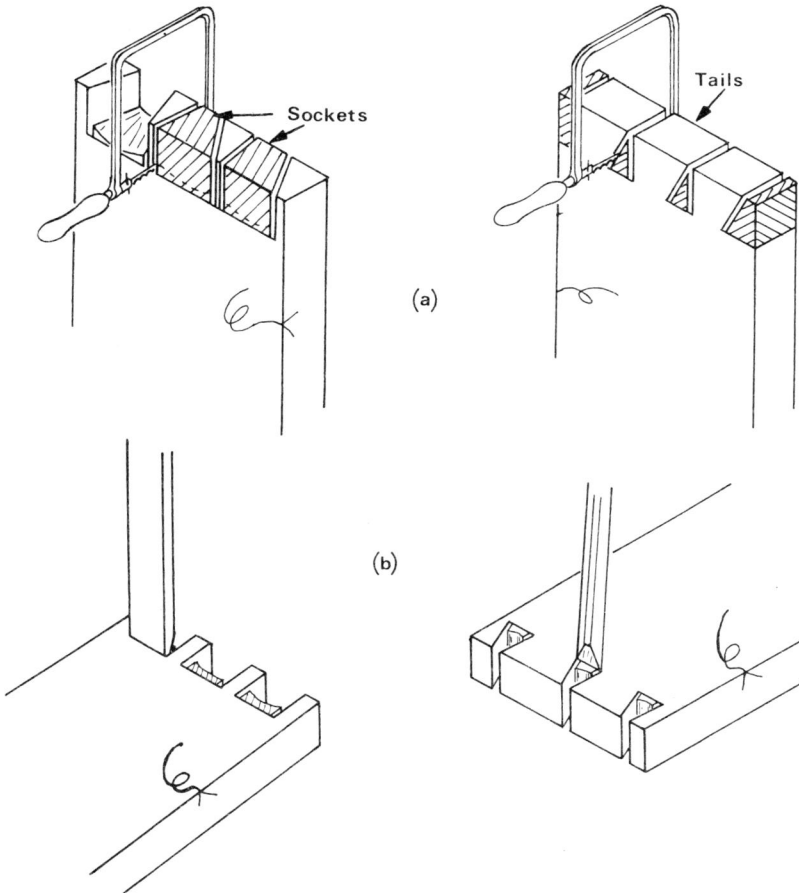

Sockets

Tails

(a)

(b)

large, then both pieces of waste may be cut out with a coping saw. When
major parts of waste are removed by sawing, each piece is laid flat with
adequate support and a firmer chisel and mallet are used to chop socket
seats square and to clear spaces between tails. If all cuts have been accurately made then the joint will fit. If dovetail joints are not accurately cut
then there is not much that can be done. Tails may be eased, but if square
abutment shoulders are not sawn away to line up with the chiselled bottoms, then easing cuts here will only make the fit less tight. See Fig. 25.

7 Shaping to Section

Shaping can be dived into two main fields of work although the two fields often overlap. This chapter deals with shaping planed lengths of wood into sections. A 'section', geometrically, is a cross, or end view, of a piece of material. If we cut a thin slice from the end of a length of planed material and draw round it, this is the section. The other field of shaping means the physical cutting and shaping of large pieces of wood to make curved shapes such as chair back rails.

Most factory woodworkers have their sections shaped up by machine, but many on-site carpenters or joiners, and many one-off cabinet makers find it more economical to run up their own shapes using hand tools or hand-held electric tools.

The home woodworker also has a choice. He can design his project around the standard stock sections that most 'Home Handyman' shops carry, or he can use his skill and prepare his own mouldings from planed square stock. The most common practice is to obtain standard stock sections.

However, should the correct sections not be available, the home woodworker is thrown back on his own resources.

SHAPING TOOLS

The first of these tools is the RABBETING plane. This consists of a light cast-iron body incorporating a comfortable hand grip. From the front, the casting may be said to be 'L' shaped, with the working sole machined flat and smooth. The vertical side seen to the left is machined smooth and flat, and is at 90° to the sole. Along the internal angle between sole and side there are two sloping cutter seatings. The pitch angle is 45° and the plane iron is used bevel down. The first cutter seating is close to the nose of the plane to enable close working into corners of frames or into stopped rabbets. It is not comfortable to use this position for general work for the toe tends to dig in. The iron does not have a separate cap iron and lever cap, but the cap provided fits sufficiently close to the cutting edge to give some degree of chip breaking. The cap fits by screw slot and is held by the opposing force of a knurled screw set at the top end of the cap. Cutting thickness (iron projection) is controlled by an adjusting lever that operates from grooves cut into the back of the iron. Some models have a screw adjuster rather than the lever.

On the smooth side of the plane there is a small projecting casting which acts as a depth stop to limit the distance to which the plane can go in depth. Set close down to the line of the sole there is a small spur which, when rotated to its cutting position, scribes a sharp line along the wood surface just before the cutting edge of the iron begins to cut. This is used when cutting rabbets across grain and avoids the necessity of using a cutting gauge.

On the opposite of the plane there is an adjustable fence, set parallel to the plane body. Thus the plane, correctly set, can cut any rabbet up to the width of the plane iron to the depth set by the depth stop. With the fence and depth stop removed the plane may be used as a shoulder plane although it is not so effective for this job as the true shoulder plane; its pitch angle is too high. The iron runs the full width of the sole.

In use, the plane is set for rabbet size and work is commenced at the distant end of the work piece. Firm control is essential to avoid rock from side to side. Each shaving is started slightly further back than the preceding one. Thus the rabbet gets deeper at a slight angle to the work-piece surface. Finally, full length shavings are removed.

The Plough

The PLOUGH plane cuts grooves, thus it is often called a GROOVING plane. Such planes are made in several sizes from light cast-iron castings. Most are plated with a rust proofing nickel, but with some parts chromed. Each size of plane will take a fairly wide range of grooving cutters from 4 mm ($\frac{1}{8}$ in.) up to 14 mm ($\frac{9}{16}$ in.) wide. It will plough grooves as deep as 15 mm ($\frac{5}{8}$ in.).

The main component is in the form of a vertical casting having a suitable hand-hold at its rear end. Unlike most other planes, its sole is not wide; it is fashioned as a thin strip, as narrow as the most narrow groove the plane will cut. Towards the plane front, on its right hand side when held in the right hand, there is an adjustable depth stop. On the left there is the running fence, adjustable on steel rods. The fence casting is shaped to provide a convenient grip for the left hand. The cutters are used bevel down and are held in by the action of small slipper-shaped cap iron and knurled finger screw. They are held in alignment with the running strip (sole) by a set screw that engages into a groove cut across the cutter back.

The plough is used in a similar manner to the rabbet plane, each groove being commenced at the far end of the work piece. If grooves wider than the widest cutter are required two cuts are made, but the first must be made with the fence set at the greatest distance. The second will require the fence moved in. Should grooves wider than twice the width of the cutter be required, then three cuts could be made, with the centre one last. Alternatively, a shoulder plane could be used to remove the centre strip.

Moulding Planes

Shop joiners at one time carried a full stock of MOULDING planes. Today, in industry, their use is non-existent, for machines produce most sections.

The bench joiner will use hand-held powered tools for much of his essential shaping. However, there are many of these wooden moulding planes about, in second-hand shops, in the boxes of older, retired joiners, and they may be found if searched for hard enough. The full range is large, covering most of the mouldings used in Victorian times. The woodworker today would use only those for the simple hollows, rounds and quirks that are reasonable to use today.

Moulding planes are of solid beechwood, with some having a hardwearing boxwood strip inserted to maintain shape. The irons are ground to shape and sharpened with slip stones. The sole of the plane is moulded by machine to the reverse of the section required. The iron is ground also to this shape. The cutters are held into the plane by a wooden wedge; there is no cap iron so shavings tend to be strong and care in use is essential.

In use, a line is pencilled on the fore end of the plane to indicate correct vertical so that the plane may be held in correct relationship to the workpiece.

Scratch Stocks

Many small sections may be scratched using SCRATCH STOCKS. These are made by the woodworker himself. They may be simple blocks for one job or they may be based on the standard marking gauge with a stem and sliding stock. The cutting tool is usually part of a broken hacksaw blade which has been ground to shape. Quite large mouldings may be built up using these but they are laborious in use. The scratch stock is very useful for the fine woodworker who wishes to inlay veneer lines etc. Fig. 26 shows simple scratch stocks in use.

PRODUCING SECTIONS

The required section is drawn on to both ends of the work piece and gauged lines are run along the length both on the sides and on top. These lines act as guides and also ensure sharp edges. The standard approach is to use rabbeting planes and grooving planes first where possible as these have guide fences.

Rabbets larger than the full width of the available plane may be made fairly easily if a groove is first ploughed to form the inner shoulder of the rabbet. Then a smoothing plane is used to remove the remaining wood. Ovolo mouldings, which are used on many window frames, are a part of an arc, and two short lines at right angles. For these, and without a moulding plane, two shallow rabbets are made on the workpiece corner. Then the sharp corner is removed by the shoulder plane. Final sanding with a shaped

Fig. 26.

a Scratch stocks have simple, squared-edged cutters, shaped to required section. They may be moved in either direction.
b Inlaid lines in veneers are easily positioned using a scratch stock.
c A boxwood line on this bowed cabinet door separates the edge banding veneer from the quartered facing.

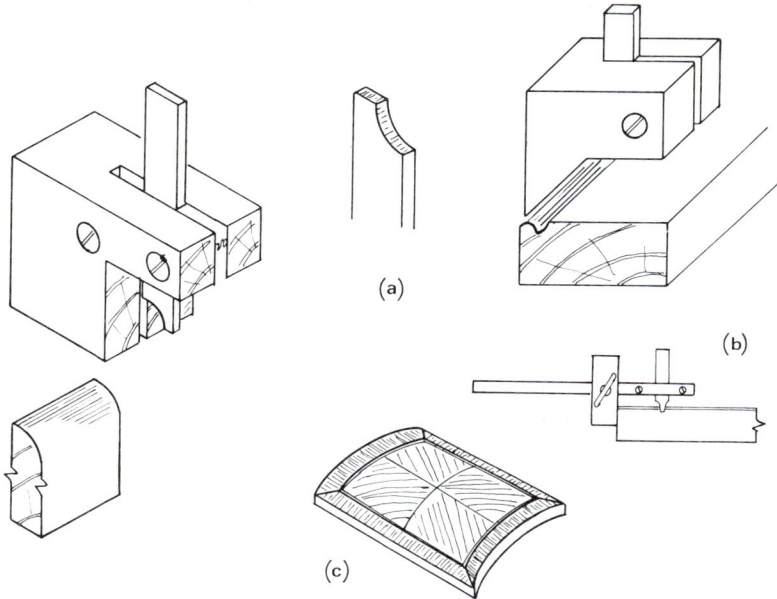

(a)

(b)

(c)

cork block will give the section required. For perfection and repetition, a scratch stock could be used to scratch the final shape after planes have removed the bulk of the wood.

Bevels are put on with smoothing planes (or block planes if across grain). With bevels and chamfers, gauge lines are not used, for a gauged line cuts into the material, whereas a bevel blends two surfaces together on a sharp corner. Pencil lines are run along for bevels.

Wooden moulding planes may sometimes be guided by fixing fences to the work with panel pins.

Another method of producing mouldings is to build them up. Here, the main tools are the rabbeter to make the tongues and the plough to make the grooves. In this way simple sections may be combined to make more complex ones. Moreover, one simple moulding may be 'planted', that is glued and pinned, to another, to make a larger moulding.

Holding The Work

One of the problems of shaping sections is that of work holding. Larger pieces may be held in the vice or simply butted against the bench stop, but smaller pieces cannot be held in this way.

Fig. 27.

a The cabinet top or table edge moulding at the top of the page may be worked in stages 1, 2 and 3.

At 1, the lines are gauged. At 2, the rabbets are made. At 3, the nosing is formed using a shoulder plane, sandpaper and block.

b Large rabbets may be made if groove is first ploughed and then the rest is removed with a smoothing plane. This is shown at 4 and 5.

c The shoulder or rabbet plane may be used for more complex mouldings. A chamfer is planed first, to gauged lines (6). Then the rabbeter is used to cut suitable rabbets (7). Finally the moulding is shaped by scratch stock and shaped cork sanding block.

d Mark out and gauge (1). Use rabbeter and shoulder plane (2).

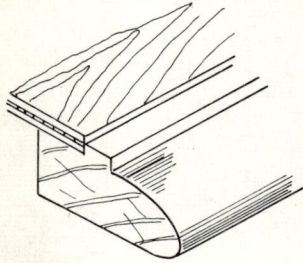
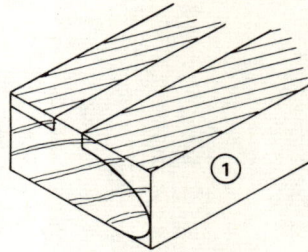
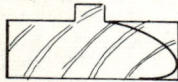

(a)

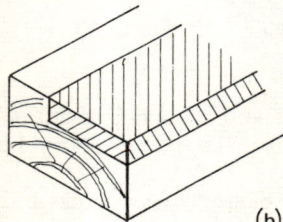

(b)

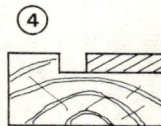
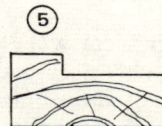

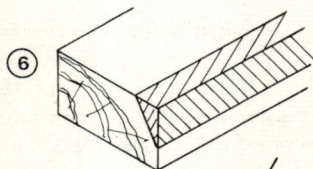

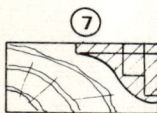
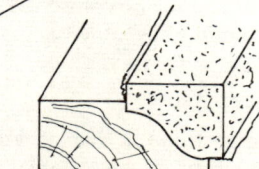

(c)

(d)

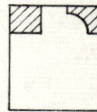
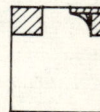

78

Fig. 28.

a Sections built-up by planting. Door stops may also be planted.
b Small work may be held in sash cramps and then held in bench vice. Alternatively, small work may be held against the bench stop by end pinning or by bench knife.

c Rounds may be shaped if the square piece is held in the 'vee' box shown. As each edge is planed the work is rotated.

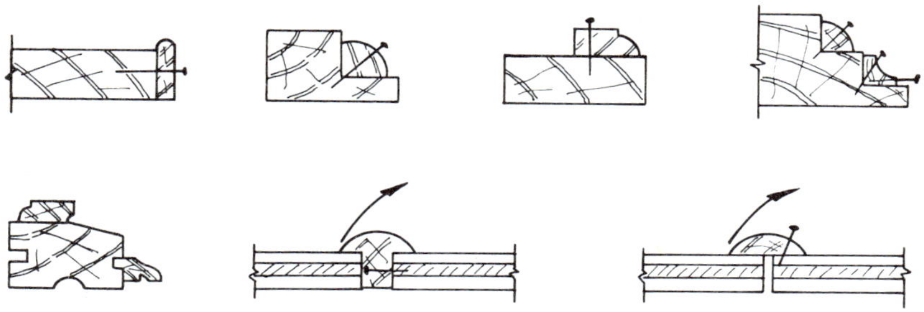

(a)

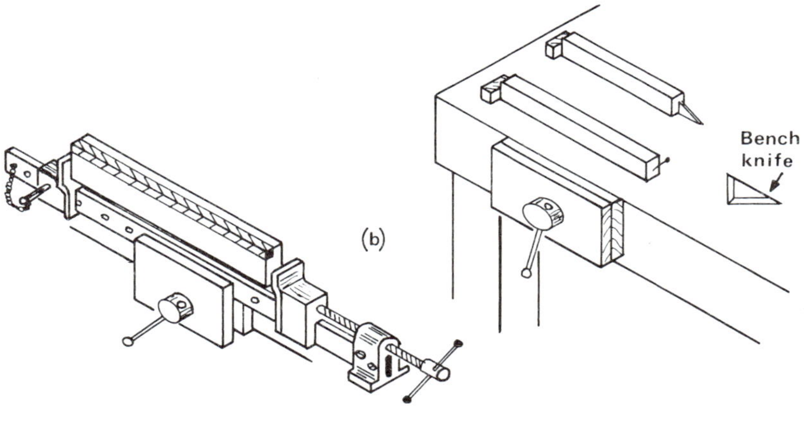

Bench knife

(b)

(c)

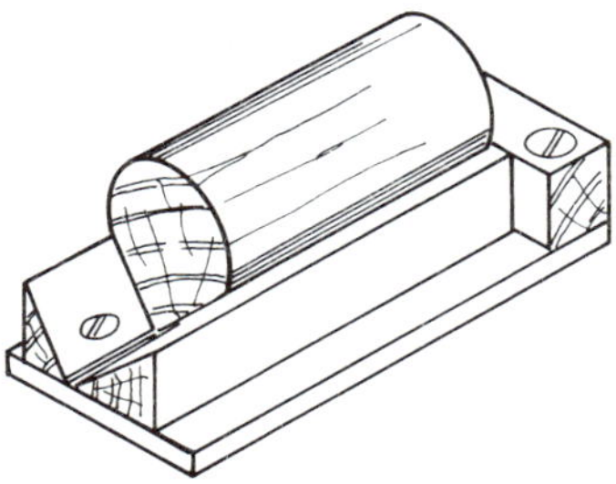

There are two general solutions. One is to butt the piece to the bench stop and to hold it there by inserting a pin through it into the bench.

The alternative is to use the SASH CRAMP, a long cramp with sliding shoe and hand screw. The work is held by the pressure of the handscrew and the locked sliding shoe. The cramp bar is then cramped into the bench vice.

Fig. 27 illustrates methods of working sections, and Fig. 28 shows planted mouldings and the method of work holding.

8 Shaping to Shape

Wood is easily shaped. From the simple flat shaping of table corners to the most complex wood sculptures, it is only a matter of using, as far as is possible, the correct tools in the correct manner. The true wood carver, or sculptor, has, of course, the other abilities of the seeing eye and the creative mind. He must create the job in his mind and search for the wood that has just the right properties of feel, of texture, and of grain to enable him to further his creative thought. His tool technique is important but it is not necessarily of greatest importance. The home woodworker may well have a degree of artistry, but his main aim is usually to produce a job that performs a function and so he must learn of the tools and of the techniques that will fulfil his functional requirements.

The saws used to shape wood have been described in earlier chapters; their use is included here. The compass plane has also been described, but the other smoother of shaped wood, the SPOKESHAVE, has not.

THE SPOKESHAVE

The Spokeshave gets its name from its original coachbuilding job of shaping wheel spokes. It is a two handed tool with the cutting edge in the centre between the hand grips. The earlier verions were made from beechwood. Imagine a rod about 255 mm long (10 in.) with the two ends shaped for convenient grip for about one third of the total length. The centre one third is cut away to form a mouth and chip escapement. At either end of this mouth there is a small square hole. The cutting iron is flat and narrow and has two upturned spikes which knock into the square holes. The cutting edge, when fully knocked home, lies flush with the face of the spokeshave. By manipulation, the tool can be pushed away from the woodworker, cutting a fine shaving as it goes. The sole may be flat or rounded. Flat-faced spokeshaves are for straight or outside curves, and the round-faced spokeshaves are for hollow or inside curves. By rotating the tool, fine or heavy cuts may be made. The cutter may be tapped out, or in.

The metal version has more elaborately shaped handles and has a cap iron and adjustable cutter. Adjustment is by two knurled finger screws which have collars that fit into slots in the iron. The lighter versions have no adjuster, the iron being moved by tapping after the hold-tight screw has been slightly released. Metal spokeshaves are also made flat or round-faced.

Spokeshaves are very much a tool for skilled use. Three fingers of each hand grip the handles, the two thumbs steady the back of the cutting portion, and the two extended fingers hold down the leading edge. With curly grained timber a slight shear angle is given to the tool. Metal spokeshave irons are pushed into a saw-cut in the end of a wooden batten to hold them when sharpening.

SHAPING

For other than single shapes developed by eye, a plywood templet is essential. This is cut accurately using a bow or fretsaw and then cleaned up to the line by the use of spokeshave, file and sanding block. After cleaning, the templet is used to mark out all of the work (such as four table legs).

The templet is applied to the planed surface and the waste side of the line indicated by shading. If the work is thick then squared lines across its thickness will enable the templet to be applied to both faces. This assists accuracy in sawing.

Sawing is done by whatever means are available, using fret, bow or compass saw. Internal perforations may be made by pre-boring and insertion of the pad saw or of the blade of one of the tension saws. If a small bench-mounted electric bandsaw is available, so much the better.

Sawing should be as far as is possible, downwards, turning the work rather than the saw. Where two lines intersect, cut the shallow cut first to avoid trapping the saw. Heavy cuts that are almost straight may be made with panel saws. In some instances, the application of a heavy chisel and mallet will speed up pre-shaping.

Having sawn or otherwise pre-shaped the work, cleaning is commenced. A wide bevel chisel is used to pare away sawing irregularities and then the most suitable planing tool is used. This may be the compass plane, smoothing plane, spokeshave or bullnose plane. The block plane (and other flat sole planes) may only be used on outside shapes.

Shapes should be cleaned with the grain, working from both ends of curves. Frequent checks must be made with the try square across the surface if squareness is required. Small curves may be pared down with gouges (scribing gouges) and internal corners pared with bevel chisels. Subject to availability, forstner bits may be used to generate very clean curves whose arcs coincide with the radius of the bit.

Finally, some smoothing and shaping may be done with a proprietary range of tools known as 'Surforms'. These are perforated hard steel sheets formed into file-like tools, each with its most appropriate handle. Some are similar to small planes, others to rasps or files with flat or rounded faces. The tools cut because the perforated faces are crimped in such a manner as to present the sharp edges of the perforations as cutting teeth. One off, small shapes such as the haft of an axe or chopper, may often be shaped entirely by Surform.

The last job is sanding. Where the standard cork block will not fit, special blocks may be shaped and the abrasive paper fitted round them.

Figs. 29, 30 and 31, illustrate many of the above points related to shaping.

Fig. 29.

a The shaped leg shown here is cut progressively from 1 to 9. The panel saw is used for 2 and 3.
The coping saw for cuts 4, 5, 8 and 9. The tenon saw is used for cuts 6 and 7. The two pieces are nailed together after cut 3.

b The half-round frame may be cut as shown from 1 to 4. Straight cuts are made with the tenon saw and curved cuts with the coping saw.

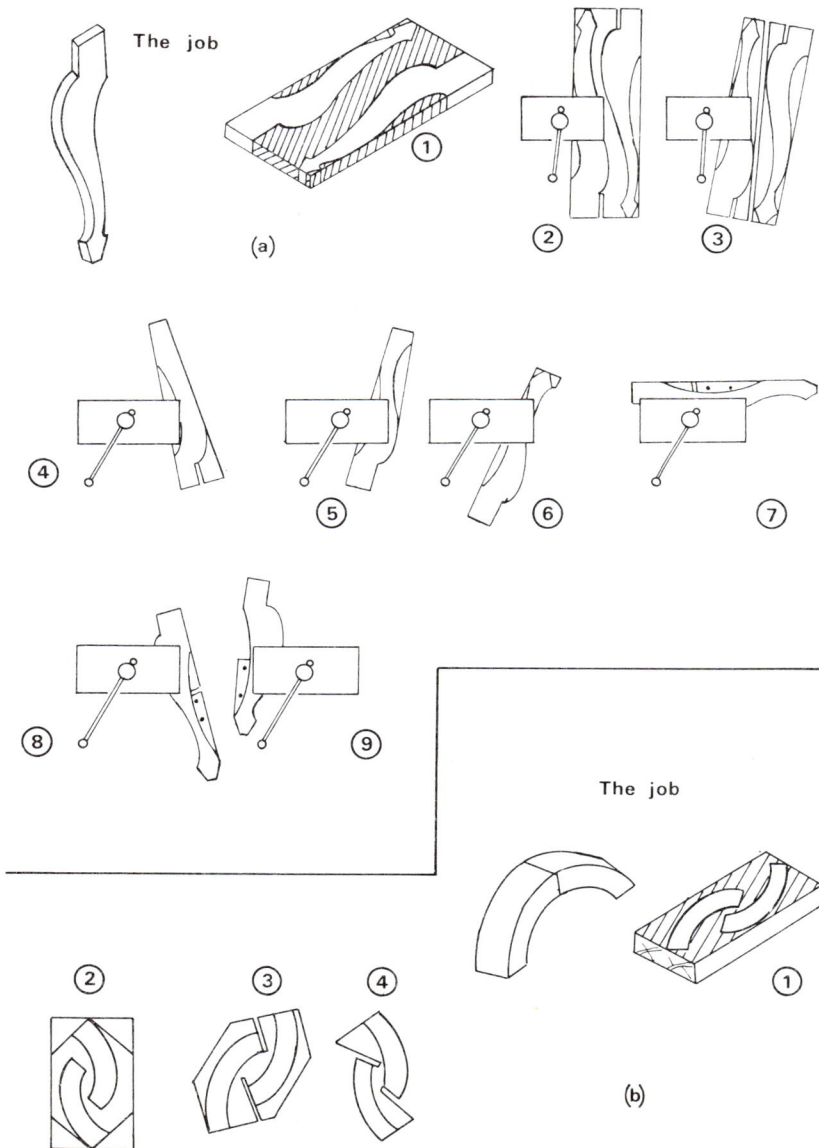

The job

(a)

(b)

The job

Fig. 30.

a Leg shown here is cut as indicated at 1 and 2.

b Chair back legs may have the wedge-shaped waste removed and then glued back on to give curve to leg.

c The shaped blocks for cabinet feet may come from the waste at the end of the rail.

d For narrow curved rails make first cut as at 1. Then glue pieces together, as at 2. Finally cut out shapes.

e Shaped post tops are first sawn to a point and then shaped with smoothing plane.

f Heavy curves are sawn, planed on their outer face and finally smoothed inside and out, with the compass plane or spokeshave, used 'down' the grain.

g Most shapes may be sawn, then cleaned into the corners with chisel or file. Final cleaning is by cork block and sandpaper.

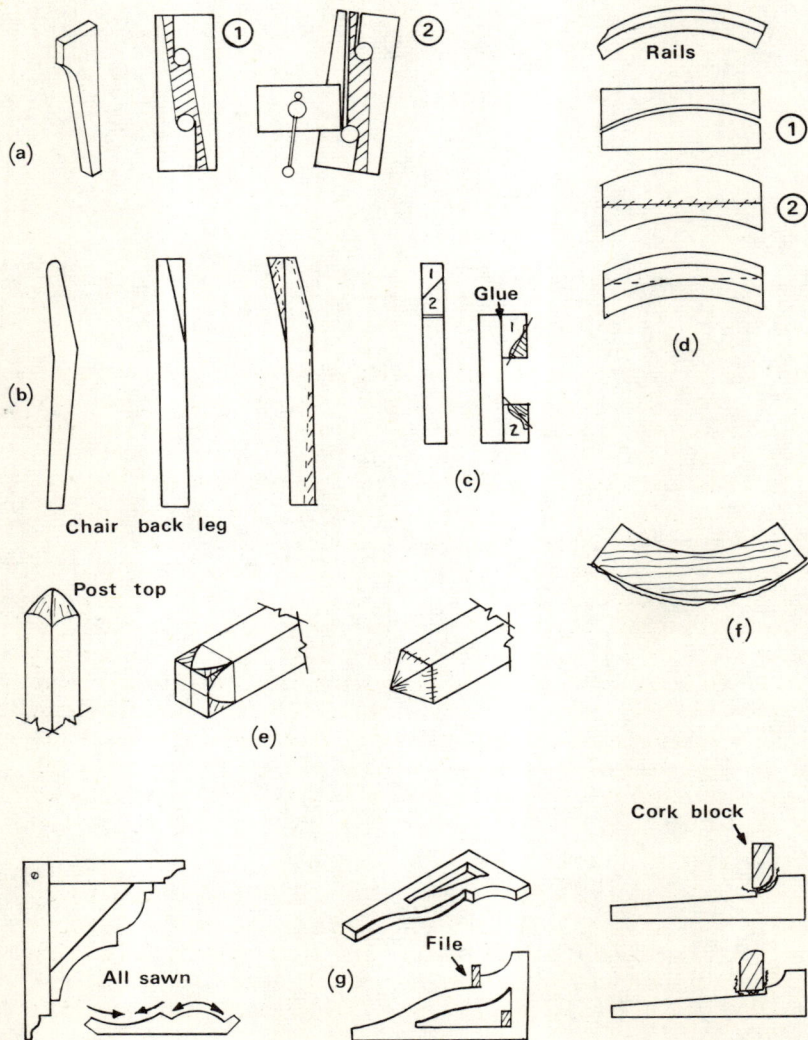

(a)

Rails

(1)

(2)

(d)

(b)

Chair back leg

Glue

(c)

(f)

Post top

(e)

All sawn

File

(g)

Cork block

Fig. 31.
a The 'Surform' range includes the plane, the flat rasp, and the round rasp and many others.
b Plywood templets are best used for marking out for shapes.
c To enlarge (or diminish) a shape use squared paper and then count squares.

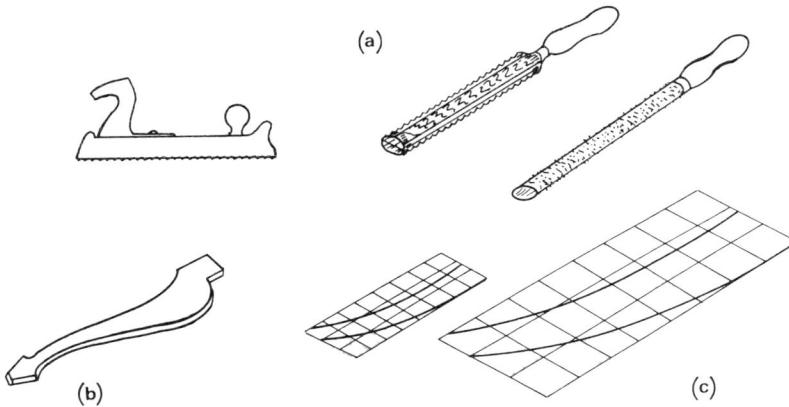

(a)

(b)

(c)

BENDING AND FORMING

Many jobs of shaping can be done by bending, especially if the wood section is small. Although home woodworkers are not likely to have the facilities to do steam bending a short statement of the principles of wood bending should be of interest.

To bend wood it must be saturated with steam or hot water. When the molecular structure is ready to slide within itself the whole piece may be bent. If it is then bent round a rigid former and cramped, it will stay close to the shape of the former when it is dry again. The process is slow and the equipment is expensive.

Home woodworkers may bend small sections or large sheets of thin ply or hardboard by pouring successive kettles of hot water on the bending area. In small boat building this technique is used, the shaped former being the ready-framed-up structure to which the skin is being applied. The bend should be left overnight cramped up to dry. When released it will maintain its shape for a sufficiently long period as to allow for the application of adhesive, when it is then finally cramped down and screwed or nailed into place.

LAMINATING

Shape forming by lamination is fairly simple but requires fairly heavy moulds. For the one-off jobs made at home the moulds would take much timber and much time. Curved drawer fronts may be made in this way if a previously-shaped pattern is available. Chair backs for subsequent veneering or upholstering are also easily made, given that a mould is available.

The process is to protect the mould with paper against glue spillage and to then glue surfaces of the ready cut laminates. (For drawers or chair backs, 4 mm plywood, laminated up to three thicknesses will do.) The glued laminates are then positioned and cramped and finally released when the adhesive has set. Only reasonably shallow bends may be made in this way and it may be necessary to pre-shape by steaming and cramping.

9 Sticking the Stuff

'Stuff' is the trade expression for pre-moulded sections drawn from stock, such as 'Sash Stuff' and 'Frame Stuff'.

When a thing is stuck it is fixed, and this is the intention—to fix firmly and to fix permanently. Rivetting, screwing and nailing are all fixings but they are not permanent—they are reversible. True glue is not reversible in the same sense. Glue may degrade, the fixing be less than permanent, but this is not the intention, it is only the result of deterioration in the joint.

ADHESIVES
Glues are ADHESIVES in that they are used to make pieces of wood adhere together—one part of a frame to another, one part of a door to another part of a door. The home woodworker has special requirements. He wants a glue that will be effective with the least possible effort and expense to himself. The glue packs sold in 'Home Handyman' shops are devised to serve the home woodworker and are restricted in range compared with those available to industry.

Adhesive Types
ANIMAL glues are usually water based and CURE (set) by evaporation of the water together with its migration to the surrounding wood. These glues are made by the boiling and treatment of animal hide, bone and hoof. They are very efficient general purpose adhesives but are reversible in that they break down if made hot or damp.

They are prepared by heating in the glue pot, when they become thin. They are applied quickly by brush and the joint is quickly cramped. Any excess is easily chiselled away when the glue is set for it becomes hard and brittle. It attains a high measure of strength before it has set off really hard. The most common woodworking animal glue is called SCOTCH GLUE.

Because of the need for clean conditions to avoid contamination, which means clean glue pots and brushes, and because of the need to heat and to apply quickly before the glue jells, Scotch glue has gone out of fashion for both home and industrial use, and only retains its popularity for veneer laying—and here only when small areas must be laid without pressing. Modern impact adhesives are taking over veneering.

PRESSING (cramping) time is about six hours to full set depending on room temperature.

Synthetic Resin
There are many of these, but most common are the ones based on UREA FORMALDEHYDE. These are non-reversible glues which have a very high resistance to moisture, heat and insect attack, and they may be used for

out-door work. They set by chemical reaction between the resin syrup and the acid (normally) hardener. The hardener is sometimes called 'the catalyst', which in chemistry, is the material which causes the varying glue chemicals to react together and become solid. The molecular movement created by the chemical reaction causes frictional heat to be generated. Synthetic resin glues cure more quickly if heated. Thus once the catalyst/hardener has been added the setting process begins and is completely non-reversible. Glues of this type are called THERMO SETTING—that is, they set by heat.

Synthetic glue is pre-packed in four forms: syrup in one can, acid hardener in a bottle; syrup in a can and hardener in powder form; glue in powder form and hardener in powder form; and finally, and the most useful of all, the resin is powder, and the hardener is powder and both are pre-mixed to form one powder. The user needs to add the pre-mixed powder to a small quantity of water, mix thoroughly and the glue is ready for use. Ideally, the creamy paste should be allowed to stand for 20 minutes after mixing before use.

The powder is stirred into the water, mixing rapidly as it is added.

Both parts of the joint are coated and the assembly is CLOSED (Cramped up). Any squeeze-out should be removed with a damp cloth, for the glue fills the grain and makes staining and polishing very difficult. Room temperatures above 20°C will accelerate cure.

POT LIFE is the time glue remains usable after mixing, and this varies from a few minutes up to about ten hours depending on room temperature and the precise nature of the glue. The one-powder type has a pot life of about 30 minutes. The pressing time is from half to about one hour, and work may be handled and worked on after about 6 hours. Full setting is reached after about 6 hours, and full strength may be reached at this time, or later if conditions are adverse. Cramping is essential, for the glue shrinks as it cures.

The working instructions on the pack must be observed.

Polyvinyl Acetate (P.V.A.)

This is a one-can glue, white and thick flowing. It is a general purpose interior glue that sets by migration of solvent into surrounding wood. It is not entirely thermo-setting and deteriorates rapidly in damp or hot surrounds. Very good for cupboards and doors but is not ideal for load carrying as in chair work. Under load and in hot conditions P.V.A. creeps from the joint and raises a fine line along it.

P.V.A. is squeezed from its plastic container and spread on to both parts of joint. Joints pressed with P.V.A. may be released for light handling after

15 to 20 minutes. Pressing is essential for strong joints but for non-load carrying structures the friction between the joint faces will suffice to hold joint together whilst glue sets. Small blocks may be glued and then rubbed together. This gives a reasonably high bond strength without cramping.

Impact Adhesives
These glues bond on impact. They are mainly for joints where large areas are in contact or for flexible joints where cramping is not possible. They are only heat and water resistant to a mild degree and resemble a cloudy yellow rubber solution. They are ideal for bonding laminated plastic sheet to chipboard and for other similar jobs.

Both parts of the job are pre-coated and are left to stand for up to 15 to 20 minutes to allow solvent to evaporate. On contact instant adhesion is secured. Mild pressure may be exerted by rubbing a smooth wooden block over the surface to make certain all parts are in contact. Because adhesion is instantaneous accurate positioning is essential and for sheet material drawing pins pushed into the side of the panel are an easy method of registration.

A variation of the impact glues is found in one that is THIXOTROPIC, which means that it has the ability to slide in shear but become jelled again if left alone. This property gives the valuable aid of 'slide' when closing the two coated surfaces together. Accurate register is not so important. It can be used quite effectively with wood veneers providing that they are reasonably flat and not cockled. Both surfaces are coated and then brought together. A hard rub with a smooth wood block will make the bond.

THE PRINCIPLES OF ADHESION
Glue sticks in two ways; by MECHANICAL ADHESION, and by SPECIFIC ADHESION.

Mechanical adhesion means that the glue penetrates the surface structure of the glued material and, in setting, produces physical 'keys' or 'interlocks'. The joint then is only as strong as the total shear strength of the combined keys. Specific adhesion relies on the affinity between one material and another. Various molecular arrangements attract similar, or approximately similar, arrangements, and when two of these approximates are brought together a molecular bond is formed.

By careful formulation, the adhesive chemists can blend materials in a manner that will give them some degree of specific adhesion to the material that is to be stuck.

The specific adhesion, together with the mechanical adhesion, provides the 'stick' between two materials.

HOME WOODWORKER'S GLUES

Resin Glues
AEROLITE 306. This is a powder resin, and acid hardeners that are coded
G.B.P. X and G.U.X. It is waterproof and must have pressure. Powder is
added to water and mixed. Hardener is applied to one side of the joint and
the resin to the other. Resin must not be mixed in FERROUS(iron) containers
otherwise some staining of wood will occur.

CASCOMITE (One-Shot). This is a white powder that contains powdered
resin and powdered hardener. The mixed powder, straight from the container, is mixed into water to make a thin paste. Both parts of joint are
coated and pressure applied. Copper, Brass or ferrous metal will cause
staining of the wood.

EVO-STIK RESIN W. is another synthetic resin glue; it is a white creamy
fluid that is coated to one part of the joint before pressure is applied.

Polyvinyl Acetate
The trade names for these vary from maker to maker and most are white
creamy fluids that are emulsions (a liquid with another heavier liquid
carried in droplets). UNITIMB, CROID 843, POLYSTIK, UNIBOND. These are
all suitable for general woodworking. They may be used for veneering if
pressure can be applied. They are resistant to water but not classified as
waterproof.

Impact Adhesives
These bond on contact. EVO·STIK 584 and 520, and THIXOFIX are three.
Thixofix is a non-drip thixotropic paste easily spread which allows some
positioning movement after contact.

GENERAL RULES
All adhesives must be used cleanly with as little overspill as possible. Too
much glue is wasteful and gives problems when polishing. Pot life and
closing times (time allowed after spread but before cramping) should be
observed. With P.V.A. all excess and squeezed-out glue should be allowed
to set partially before paring off with a chisel. Water washing of wet glue only
washes it into grain. With synthetic resin, excess may be removed with a
damp soapy rag.

KNOCKING-UP
Knocking-up is a trade expression embracing all the operations of glueing,
assembly and cramping. It implies that all sections are cut, shaped and
cleaned, and joints fitted. It is preceded by a 'cleaning-up' session,

90

cleaning-up the inside faces of the work, all those that will not be accessible after assembly, and all those that are not liable to damage or deterioration during assembly. Cleaning-up also means that the decks are cleared for action, all chips away, all tools returned to their proper places, and the working area ready for working with adhesives and cramps. During this preliminary period, cramping blocks are made, wedges cut, dowels trimmed and the necessary knocking up tools collected. These tools are: hammer, mallet, square, chisel, glue pot and brush, or glue dispenser, damp rag and squaring stick, together with such cramps that are available.

Cramps
Small work requires small cramps and the smallest are thumbscrews—small cramps made from pressed up flat steel with a small screw for tightening. Not much pressure can be exerted by these but they can apply quite sufficient force to keep faces in contact during the glue cure time. Spring clips are now beginning to take over some of the work from thumbscrews. 'G' cramps are castings and are in the shape of a capital 'G'. Pressure is applied by thumb screw. They range in size from miniatures at 35 mm opening, to heavy duty at 305 mm opening. They may be light section or heavy; some have quick release spinners, some have deep-reach throats. Ingenuity will find uses for 'G' cramps in work holding, joint closing and work springing gradually to pull round a thick laminate.

Not so popular, but very useful, are HANDSCREW cramps with wooden jaws and either wood or metal screws. There are two jaws and two screws. Regular closing will keep jaws parallel, but with the additional facility of metal screws and pivoting centres, out of parallel jobs may be cramped. One use for handscrews that is not available to any other form of clamp is their ability to be used in pairs as a work vice. One is laid flat on a heavy table top where it is cramped down with the other. Work may then be held firmly if the first cramp is closed.

Carcase, or box constructions, door or frame constructions need SASH cramps or the heavier versions of these called TEE-BAR cramps. They both consist of a long bar along which the cramping head slides when moved by the handscrew. At the other end of the bar to the sliding head there is the fixed shoe, which is located and locked in selected position by use of a steel dowel pin. Sash cramps have a plane rectangular bar, but tee-bar cramps have a much heavier 'T' section.

ASSEMBLY
Cramps are made ready first, for joints that have glue applied are messy and awkward to handle whilst trying to adjust cramps. Work is usually

Fig. 32.
a Improvised cramping making use of folding wedges.
b Improvised cramps to hold surfacing plywood down.
c To edge-cramp heavy boards or jobs, use the garage floor. Use bricks and battens as spacers and wedges to apply pressure.
d Table under-frames may be cramped between garage roof and bench top. Folding wedges apply pressure.
e Wooden hand-screws make a useful vice if necessary.

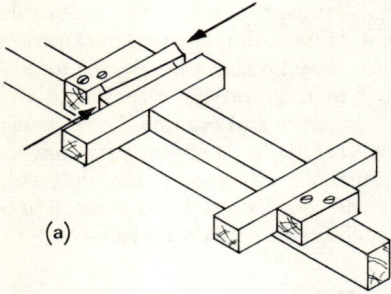

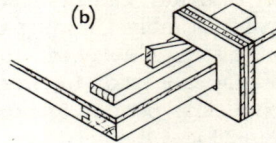

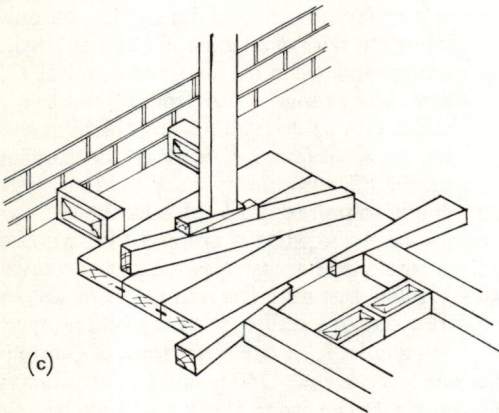

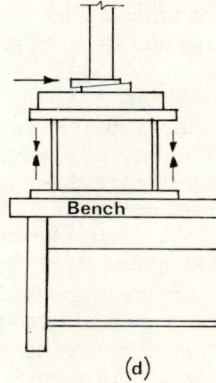

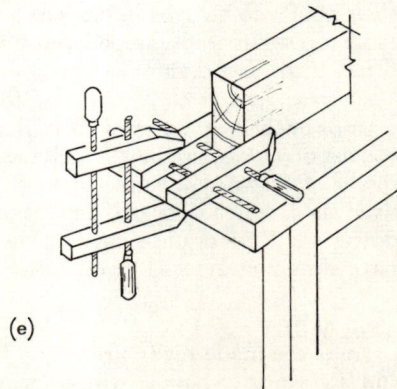

(a)

(b)

Bench

(d)

(c)

(e)

Fig. 33.

a Cramp flat frames with cramps as shown. This avoids bowing of stiles.

b A steel square may be used internally to check a frame. A nailed batten will keep frame square until required.

c Corner to corner squaring with the squaring stick gives best results, for if the diagonals are equal the frame is square.

d Viewed from the end any frame must be flat and not in-winding.

e Protect work by using ply cramp pads between cramp shoe and work.

f Sash cramps will pull frame out of (continued on following page)

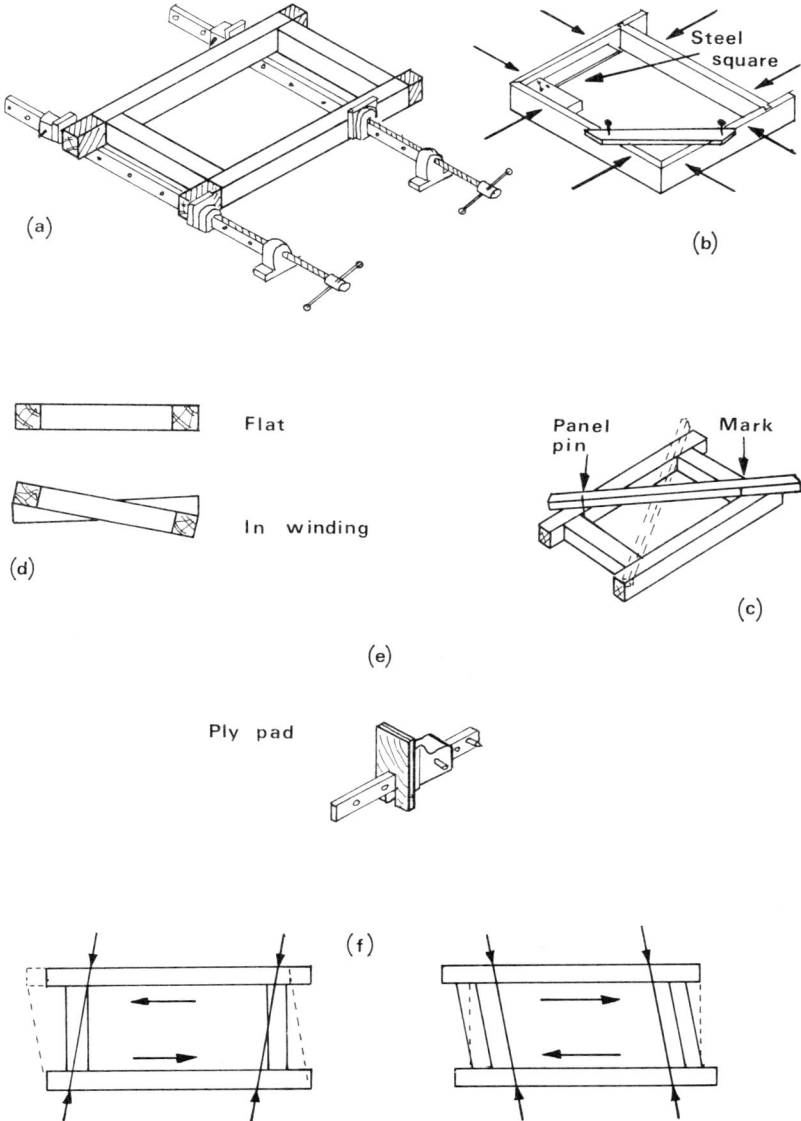

(a)

(b)

Steel square

Flat

In winding

(d)

Panel pin

Mark

(c)

(e)

Ply pad

(f)

93

square if they are not parallel to rails. If
frame is out-of-square, adjustment to the
line of the cramps will pull it back into
square.

assembled and cramped dry first for it is a bit late in the day to find that a
joint will not close after glue has been applied.

After test, the job is carefully knocked apart. All edges are protected with
small wooden blocks when they are being knocked. A hammer is best for
this as it is more easily used in closed areas and carries more impact than a
mallet.

With the cramp arranged and ready, glue is applied sparingly. Mortise
and tenon joints have glue applied to both parts. Careful attention being
given to the tenon shoulders. For work where there are several components, a procedure plan must be made. If possible sub-assembly and
glueing should be arranged, with each sub-assembled part being glued and
cramped before it is offered to the main final assembly. Such jobs would include the top section of a slotted gate where manipulation of many pieces is
difficult or the shelf divisions of a book-case unit. Plinths and table under-
frames are other examples.

Long cramps must be arranged parallel to the rail that they are cramping. Any skew on the cramp will pull the frame or whatever is being
cramped, out of square. Conversely, if the job does pull up out of square,
moving the cramps out of square will pull the job back square. Frames
must also be out-of-wind, i.e. not twisted. To check this, a sighting is made
across the top edges of two extreme rails. They should appear to merge. If
the frame is not flat, then the cramps again will pull it true.

When light frames, such as window sashes, are being pulled up, one
cramp should be on one extreme end outside of the rail, and the other
should be just inside the opposing rail. In this way any springing of the
stiles is avoided.

The first check is made with a try square, but when the job appears correct, a final check, is made across corners with the squaring stick.

Only when all is square and flat are any corner blocks or wedges fitted.
All work in cramp should remain flat whilst the glue sets.

Figs. 32 and 33 show examples of glueing techniques.

10 Fixing and Fitting

FIXING

This is the name given to the job of firmly attaching one thing to another, usually without the aid of glue. FITTING is the name given to the job of equipping a nearly finished job with all of its metalware or plastic ware such as hinges, locks, stays, brackets, handles and so on. The job of fixing also includes the permanent fixing of shelves to walls, and of hanging cupboards to walls.

NAILING

To nail, is to use a small pointed piece of metal to fasten wood or other material. Nails are designed to do specialist jobs. Most common is the FRENCH or WIRE nail, a round section, mild steel nail with a flat head. Wire nails run from 18 mm ($\frac{3}{4}$ in.) to 150 mm (6 in.). The long sizes are commonly called spikes. As their length is increased so is their diameter. A general rule is that they must always be at least twice as long as the thickness of the material they are fastening. For exterior work they may be galvanised.

Wire nails are used for general work in the rougher type of woodwork where the large round heads are not a drawback.

OVAL nails are also correctly named as wire nails, but this name is not often used. They are oval in section and have deep heads, rather like a thickening of the wire. The spread out flat head of the french nail is missing and so ovals are more easily driven in and filled to avoid unsightliness, They again run from 18 mm to 150 mm. Being oval, they tend to open grain lines with a minimum of disruption and are not so likely to split when used close to ends of a board.

For floor-board fixing, CUT FLOOR·BRADS are used. These are square in section and have no head as such, only a shoulder projection. Having a square tip they punch a fairly clean hole through the floor board without splitting. They are of black mild steel. In size they go from 35 mm to 75 mm ($1\frac{1}{2}$ in. to 3 in.). A slightly lighter version may sometimes be found, called the JOINER'S BRAD. The head of the nail must always line up with the wood grain.

For general carpentry (structural woodwork) use CLASP nails. These are square in section and have shouldered heads that are easily driven in flush. They are made up to 180 mm long.

There are so many other types of construction nails that only very few get into general use.

For lighter work such as the attachment of mouldings and for fastening housings in light jobs etc. PANEL PINS are used. These are slender in section and round. Their heads are flat but tapered into the nail shank. In length they are made from 9 mm to 50 mm ($\frac{3}{8}$ in. to 2 in.). They are of bright mild steel. A more slender version is the VENEER PIN which has a more buttressed head and is of a very fine round section. Veneer pins are essential for the attachment of slim section mouldings and for jobs that are glued, but require firm fixing whilst glue is setting. They may be punched in and filled or they may be left with the head proud so that they may be pulled out when the glue is set. Veneer pins are made from 9 mm to 35 mm.

Jobs that are to be nailed into building structures require nails made of hardened steel. These cannot be driven into concrete and to attempt to do so is dangerous. The nails fly away if they are hit and this is painful to fingers and puts the eyes and face at risk. These hard pins, sometimes called MASONRY PINS, are stouter in GAUGE (diameter) than normal nails of the same length. Care in use is essential, for brickwork varies in hardness and too heavy use of a hammer will split the brick (or breeze block). If it is necessary to obtain a fixing into concrete by nailing, a hole should be made and plugged and nails may be driven into the plugs.

HARDBOARD (a pressed woodpulp board), is fixed with hardboard pins. These are either zinc-plated panel pins or square section copper-plated tingles. Tingles, are, in general, very sharp and very slender, cut nails. The hardboard pin is driven into the board and its head is lost in the surface without punching. The small hole left is often sufficiently filled by subsequent paint.

Another special nail is the STAR nail, a star-section nail that is now often used for production joinery. It is driven through mortise and tenon and bridle joints, and left flush with the surface where it shows as a small cross. Painting covers it.

NAILING METHODS

Never nail closer to an edge or end than is necessary. Use only the nail that is suited for the job. A long, large nail, is no stronger than a slender one if it splits the material.

When very slender work is to be nailed, or if nails must go close to an end, then before nailing, the pin or nail has its point made flat by means of a hammer blow onto its point with its head placed on the vice cheek or similar hard material.

A glued and pinned job should have the pins driven into one piece of the job first. Then when the glue is applied a light tap quickly holds the job whilst it is finally lined up. If a secretly nailed job is required then a pocket is prized open prior to the nail insertion. The flap is then glued back after the nail is punched in.

For jobs that may later be taken apart the nail heads are left proud and the nails are driven straight in. Skew nailing increases the holding power but also increases the risk of bent nails.

To conceal nails in joinery work their heads are punched in and the holes are filled with putty or POLYFILLA, a modern plaster-like white powder that is mixed with water. To avoid rust the nail head and hole may first be painted with an undercoat. The filler is knifed in and sanded flat when dry. Polished jobs have pins punched in and the holes filled with proprietary stopping, after which the job is stained and polished. Nails and nailing methods are shown in Fig. 34.

SCREWS
Screws are reversible fixings, they may be taken out if the job has to be dismantled. They are more rigid, and strong when correctly used, than nails. * *except in end-grain* The most commonly used variety are BRIGHT MILD WOOD SCREWS. For quality joinery and cabinet work, brass screws are used, but these are much weaker and require careful handling. For screws that are visible chromium-plated heads are available. Weather resistant screws are BLACK JAPPED; these are mainly round headed.

Screw Types
Screws are named by their head formation. There are COUNTERSUNK heads, RAISED heads, ROUND heads and PHILLIP heads.

Countersunk heads are flat on top but chamfered underneath. They are used in countersunk holes and lie flush, or just below, the surface. Raised heads have a slightly moulded head that is countersunk below. It is these that are most often plated for appearance. Round heads have a fully domed head that is flat underneath. They are most obtrusive in use and require careful use of screwdriver to avoid slot burring.

Phillip head screws are mainly countersunk screws, having a central star-hole rather than the traditional slot of the standard screw. A similar variety has the name POZIDRIV. Both these, the Pozidriv and the Phillips require their own patented screwdriver.

USE OF SCREWS
Screws hold by the compressive force exerted between their heads and the worm of their screw. It is essential to obtain maximum area of cover for their heads and the maximum bite for their worms.

For good screw fixing a clearance hole must be drilled in the part to be fixed, and a thread hole drilled into the part that is to take the screw thread.

The clearance hole should be fractionally larger than the shank diameter of the screw and the thread hole be approximately half of the diameter of the clearance hole. Thus a screw with a shank of 6 mm diameter would need a thread hole of about 3 mm. These dimensions are variable;

Fig. 34.
a 1. Wire nail, 2. Oval nail, 3. Cut brad, 4. Clasp nail, 5. Panel pin, 6. Veneer pin, 7. Masonry pin, 8. Hardboard pin, 9. Star nail, 10. Nail length must be twice thickness of material being fastened.
b Nails close to ends split wood; flattening the point helps to prevent this.
c Pinning methods: conceal pins into corners; space nails regularly for ply bottoms; pin mitres from both sides; dovetail nails for greater holding power; conceal nails under a small flap if necessary. For temporary holding leave heads proud for extracting; Clench nails back into wood for greater strength when work is external.

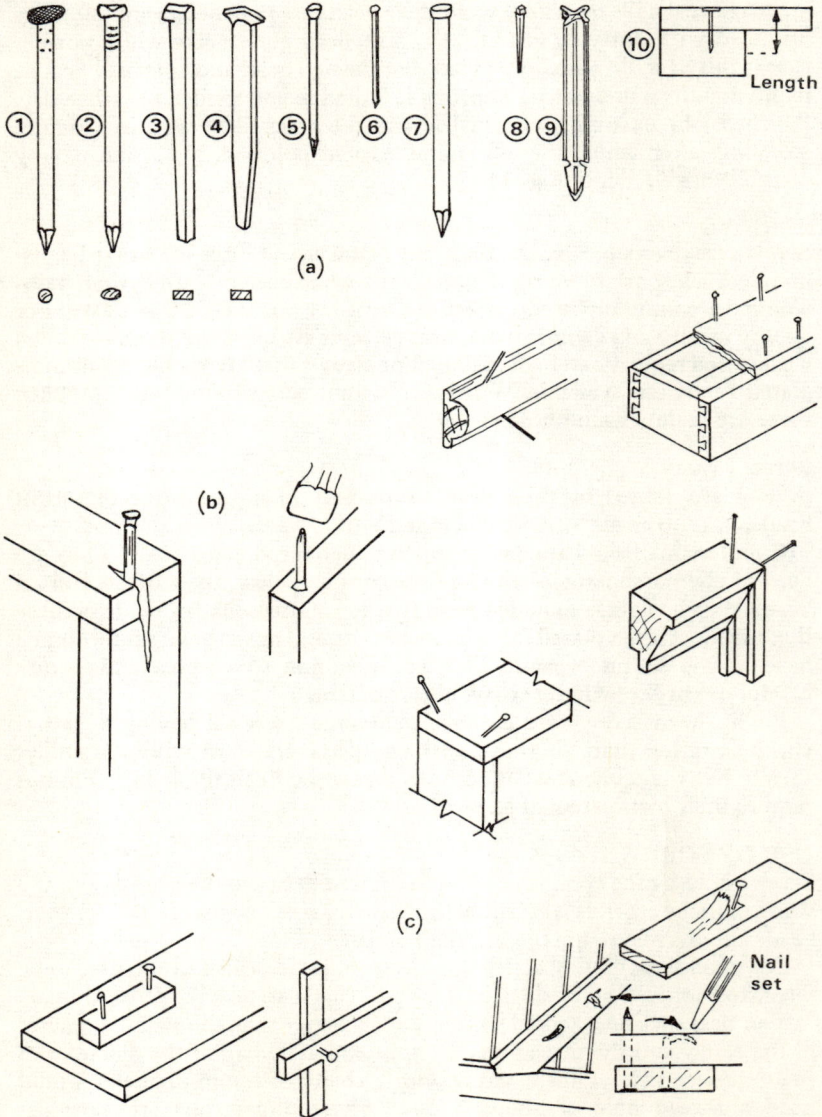

(a)

(b)

(c)

softwoods being more tolerant of variation than brittle hardwoods. Screw manufacturers produce charts that contain the relevant dimensions of all screws and the holes necessary for their use. Screw sizes are given in length and gauge. The length is overall and the gauge is the shank gauge size. The most popular range for cabinet type work runs from No. 2 up to No. 6. TWOS, as they are called, are about 2.4 mm dia. and SIXES are close to 4 mm. Joinery and carpentry screws run from No. 4 up to No. 14. (FOURS about 3.2 mm and FOURTEENS about 6.4 mm). Screw lengths run from 6 mm up to 150 mm, but all gauges are not available in all lengths.

Screw length must be related to the holding power of the material into which the screw is inserted and the gauge size to the thickness of the material being fixed. This is a general rule and the user must use common sense in application. To fix unglued 4 mm plywood to a softwood backing a 18 mm ($\frac{3}{4}$ in.) No. 4 would be suitable. To fix the same ply, glued, to a hardwood frame a 12 mm ($\frac{1}{2}$ in.) No. 3 would do, or even the smaller and shorter 9 mm ($\frac{3}{8}$ in.) No. 2 for cabinet work. For screws carrying a heavy pulling load, large gauges are necessary, for the larger the gauge, the better is the fixing against direct pulling.

Brass screws are weak in shear. Adequate pre-boring is essential and if dealing with hardwoods, a steel screw should be screwed into the hole first then extracted.

Never run the finger across a newly driven screwhead to feel whether it is flat. Screw drivers sometimes leave an extremely sharp wire splinter on screw heads and the practice of 'brushing' drives these splinters into the fingers.

CARPENTRY FIXING

Nuts, Bolts, Coach Screws and Coach Bolts
Nuts and bolts are usually hexagonal and are used for roofing work and general heavy fixing where access is possible to both sides of the job. Holes are pre-bored into both pieces to be fixed and the bolts are threaded through with washers at either end to protect the wood. Between the timber members there are circular, toothed, timber connectors. Coach bolts have round heads with a short square section immediately below the head. The bolt shank is round. Holes are pre-bored and the bolt is threaded through but with no washer, and as the nut is pulled home, the square shank head bites and prevents the bolt from turning. These bolts are often counter bored below the surface for an improvement in appearance.

Coach screws are heavy screws with square heads that are turned into the job by spanner. Large thread holes are essential. Screw types, together with usage are shown in Fig. 35.

Fig. 35.

a 1. Countersunk woodscrew; 2. Raised head; 3. Round head; 4. 'Pozidriv' and Phillips head; 5 and 6. Surface and countersunk screw cups.

b Good screwing requires three hole pre-boring: 1. Counter-sinking; 2. Shank clearance; 3. Pilot hole.

c Wood is countersunk; Metal requires round heads. Screws may be 'pocketed' for concealment.

d Screws pushed into grease-filled matchboxes are always ready for use. Polished wood surrounds may have (*continued on following page*)

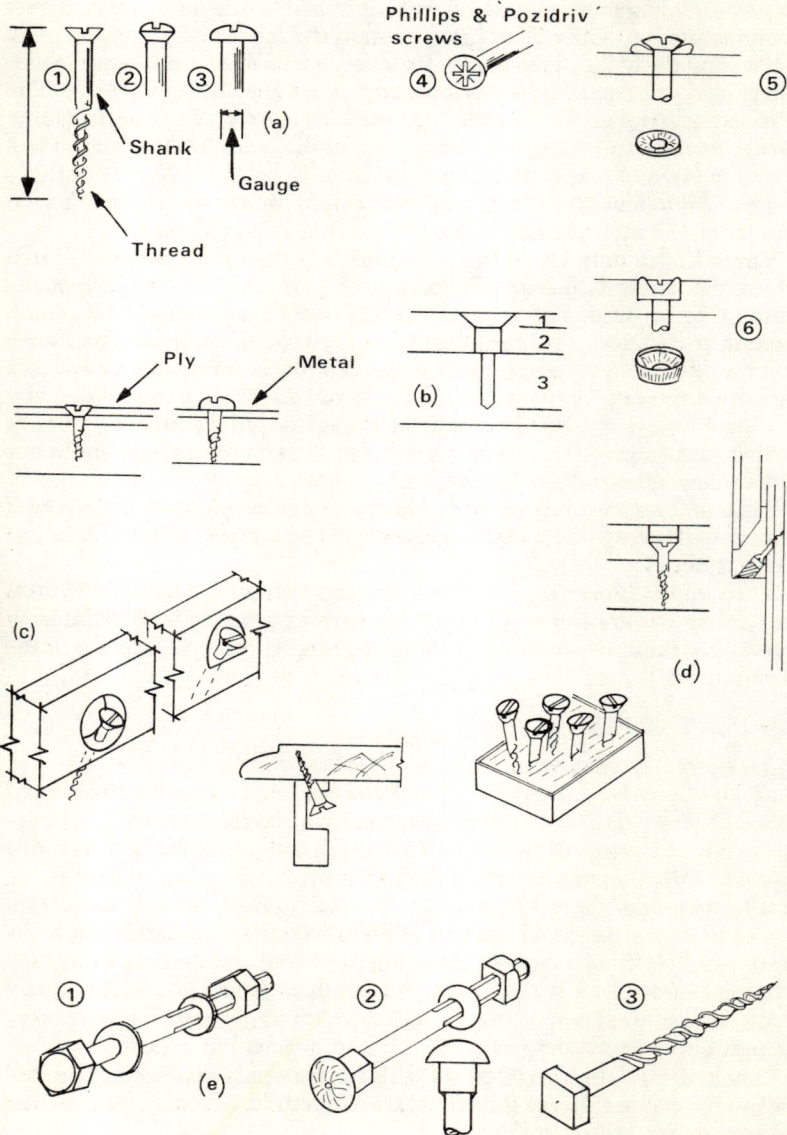

Shank

Gauge

(a)

Thread

Phillips & Pozidriv screws

④

⑤

Ply

Metal

1
2
3

(b)

⑥

(c)

(d)

① ② ③

(e)

screws concealed with wood pellets.
e 1. Nut, bolt, and washers, for heavy
       fixing.
   2. Coach bolt for sheds, fences, roofs
       etc.
   3. Coach screw for bench tops and
       decking.

TOOLS USED FOR FIXING

First and foremost is the hammer. The hammer operates by impact. The effort applied to the handle, the centrifugal force generated during its swing, and the momentum built up during the movement are all expended as kinetic energy at the second of impact. The force thus generated drives in the nail being hit. Square hitting is essential to obtain maximum impact drive.

The four hammers likely to be of general use are the WARRINGTON, the CLAW, the PIN and the CLUB.

The Warrington is the general purpose woodworker's hammer. It has a round, flat, striking head and a narrow, flat pein. The pein is the opposite end to the striking end of any hammer, and is used for jobs that the normal striking end cannot reach. Warringtons are sold in sizes, each size code reflecting the weight of the head. A No. 4 Warrington weighs 16 oz. and the No. 2, which is the average, weighs 12 oz.

The Claw hammer has a flat, round, striking head, but no pein. The opposite end to the striking end is shaped as a claw and is intended for the extraction of partly driven nails. The claw hammer tends to be heavier than the Warrington, and a No. 4 weighs 24 oz. The Pin hammer is a lighter version of the Warrington and has a larger, more slender pein and weighs from 4 to 6 oz.

The club hammer is a heavy impact hammer, and is used for general building and driving work. Bricklayers use it, together with a bolster chisel to split bricks. It has an approximately rectangular head with driving faces at either end. It has a short stout handle. Club hammers are made in $2\frac{1}{2}$ lb., and 4 lb. sizes.

Screwdrivers

Screwdrivers drive screws. Or they should, but if the drive end, the bit, does not correctly fit the screw slot, both screw and work will be damaged. To cover all sizes of screwdriver is not possible, so to compromise, the industrious home woodworker will probably need: a heavy driver with a round or hexagonal grip, with the blade having a nut fashioned to its ferrule. This is known as a MECHANICS screwdriver. A lighter driver that has an oval, or egg shaped handle in wood or plastic, is called a cabinet driver. For small screws an electrician's driver is useful. This has a long slender blade with an insulating plastic handle of parallel section.

Screwdrivers are graded by length with the average use model being 305 mm overall.

Special drivers for Phillips and Pozidriv screws are similar in pattern to cabinet drivers but have their own special bit ends and have shorter and stouter shanks.

For quantity screwing the YANKEE or PUMP driver is used. This has a spiral ratchet blade that rotates the bit as effort is applied to the handle. Great care must be taken with these for they easily slip from the screw and mark the work. Similarly, to speed the insertion of many screws, a ratchet driver is used. This has a ratcheted handle that allows oscillation without release. It is very useful where one hand is needed to support part of a job such as in door-hanging and lid-fitting. Screws going into hardwood should be lightly greased or soaped before insertion.

Pincers
These extract nails. Their teeth must be kept slightly blunt to prevent the shearing off of nail heads as they are extracted. They operate on the lever principle. The hand grips the handles and closes them together. The jaws bite below the nail head. As the hand is then lowered, the jaws rotate on their outside and centre and create leverage. Direct pulling is rarely successful. A flat steel rule used close to the nail head will prevent the pincers marking the job.

Punches
These are short hard steel drive pins that have a very hard tip and a softer, tougher head. The tip sits on to the nail or pinhead and the head of the punch is dealt a hammer blow. The head end of the punch is softer than the tip to avoid marking the hammer face and to avoid the metal splintering as it is struck. Fine pointed punches are called PIN punches and heavier ones are called NAILSETS.

WALL HOLING
To drill holes into walls, either of brick or concrete, special tools are required. The hand method is to use JUMPING BITS. These are a patent 'Rawlplug' Co. tool. The tool holder is hexagonal in section and has a tapered hole in one end. This receives the bit, an approximately triangular hard steel tool with a tapered shank to fit into the handle. The complete tool is held in the left hand and struck a hammer blow. The hand then rotates the bit. In this manner, impact and rotation, holes are gradually drilled. Too heavy blows will crack concrete or brick, so a series of smart sharp blows are struck with plenty of turning movement.

Plugging chisels are used by builders to drive the mortar out from the joints of brickwork. The slots thus made are then filled by wooden plugs driven in by hammer. Either nails or screws are then driven into the plugs for fixing.

The modern method of wall holing is to use electric drills and tungsten carbide tipped bits. These bits are hard steel and very tough. Their cutting tips are made from one of the hardest materials known to man. The tip is brazed on during manufacture. When blunted after long use, these bits may be ground on special silicon carbide, or diamond impregnated grinding wheels. The silicon carbide wheels are usually green in colour and are called GREEN GRIT wheels. Such wheels may be bought to fit small mandrels driven in the electric drill.

Fast running woodworking electric drills are of no use for these tipped bits so a two speed, or single low speed drill is essential. In use tipped drills often strike hard stones and will not penetrate. In such cases several blows with a suitably sized jumper bit will often shatter the stone before drilling continues.

When drilled, the holes are plugged with RAWLPLUGS, a patented fibre plug. These have centre holes. Into these the screws are driven. As the screw penetrates the plug expands and bites into the brick of the wall and the screw is firmly held. Modern developments include plastic plugs and fibrous asbestos wool mixed with cement with the trade name of PHILPLUG.

For heavy fixing into walls, RAWLBOLTS are used. These have a malleable iron sleeve, split into two. Between these sleeves there is a loose fitting tapered bolt-head. The unit is inserted into the hole in the wall, with the bolt screwed end projecting. When the job is positioned over the bolt end, a washer and nut are threaded on.

As the nut is tightened the bolt head is pulled up through the shields. expanding them into tight grip with the sides of the holes. Fig. 36 shows fixing method.

FITTINGS

Fittings are the bits and pieces applied to wooden items to make them work. They include locks, bolts, hinges, handles, stays, slides and catches. Door equipment is known as 'door furniture'.

Plastics are taking over from metals in the manufacture of fittings, and the range of plastic fittings is enormous. Only general notes can really be included here, and details of the fittings and assembly of particular fittings must be sought from the supplier.

Hinges

Hinges are pivots. In ten minutes spent in a Home Handyman shop so many varieties of hinges may be seen that the longer one stays, the more unsure one becomes as to the correct hinge for the job. It is best to approach the job from the 'end product' angle. Define the hinge situation and the correct hinge is then fairly easily selected.

Fig. 36.
a 1. Spot wall with nail and drill hole; 2.
Drive in plug; 3. Make screw entry hole
with a nail; 4. Grease and insert screw.
b Heavy porch timbers may be fixed
with 'Rawlbolt Anchors' into which bolts
are screwed.

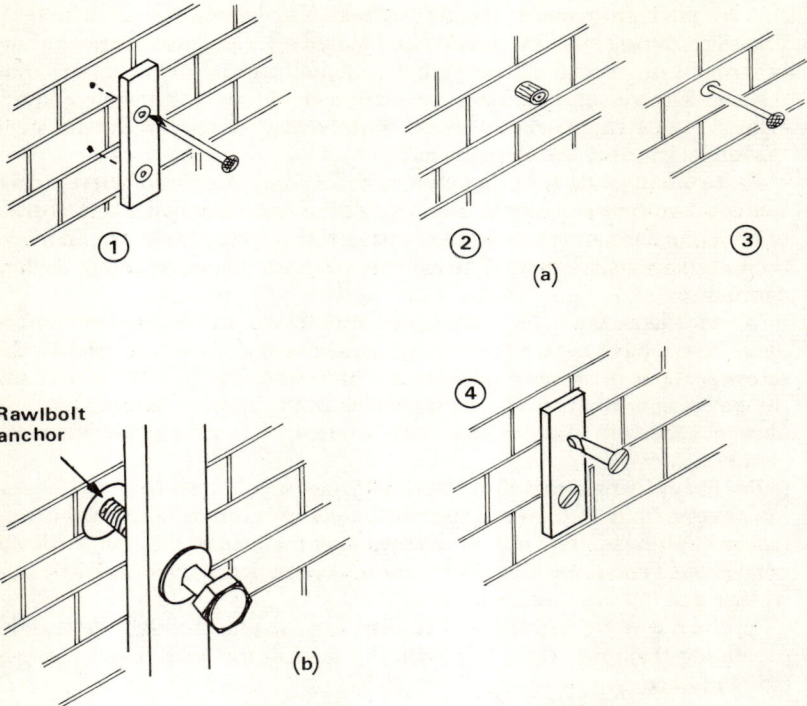

Butt Hinges

These are the most common hinge. They are used for pivoting joinery
doors and windows, and cabinet doors and flaps where the material is
strong enough to take a reasonable length screw.

Butt hinges are described by details of their construction. Standard light
door hinges are of pressed mild steel. Hardwood doors are usually fitted
with solid drawn brass hinges with steel pins and washers.

Doors to garages may be hung with cast iron butts, and these are heavy
in section and inelegant in appearance.

Butt hinge variations include types that have the two halves recessed
into each other so that only one thickness is shown and no recessing is needed
to fit them. These are known as the 'Hurlinge'. Another variation is the rising
butt. This raises the door as it opens, thus lifting it clear of the carpeted floor.
Rising butts also cause the door to be self-closing.

The 'pin hinge' is a butt hinge that has a withdrawable pin. This enables removal of the door without the need for use of a screwdriver.

Other Hinges
Other joinery hinges are: BACK FLAPS, CROSS GARNET, RABBETED, PARLIAMENT and EASY·CLEAN window types.

Back Flaps will open to about 150° but their main difference to butt hinges is that their plates are wide and square, rather than being long and narrow, and this gives a much greater fixing area. They are best used horizontally, especially the cheaper varieties, for they are intended to carry loads across the pin rather than in-line with it.

Cross-Garnets are 'T' hinges, usually blacked for weather protection. They are used for gates and matchboarded doors. Their long plate is surface fixed but the small plate may be cut into the frame rabbet. Rabbeted hinges are used either into the rabbets of storm proof windows or for surface fittings of kitchen cabinet surface mounted doors. Parliament hinges are used when doors must open to 180°, which means that the door will open into the room and back flush with the wall.

They have their pivot section made to project out from the door. Easy-Clean window hinges have an extended pivot which enables the window to swing open and away from its frame jamb leaving sufficient arm room for cleaning.

Furniture Hinges
Furniture hinges are changing in design all the time. These changes take note of new materials and new tastes in furniture design. It is not possible to tabulate types but it is possible to look at the jobs the hinges are required to do.

Changes in design are brought about by the new materials that are available. Plastics technology allows more and more fittings to be made more tasteful and elegant, more efficient, and more economic. The use of particle board makes it necessary to have other methods of fixing fittings than deep screwing, for particle board is not an ideal material for screw fixing.

HINGE SITUATIONS
Hinges may be required not to be seen, to enable wardrobe doors to open more than 90°. To allow doors to open and yet stay within the overall width of the cabinet so that two such cabinets may stand close together. To allow doors to fit between cabinet sides and yet open through 180° and still be flush with the cabinet front. To allow secure fitting into thin particle board

(15 mm). To allow a door to open through 270°, which will allow it to be folded back alongside the cabinet. To allow easy, rapid and accurate fitting by a reasonably proficient handyman.

All of these situations are catered for by furniture hinges. It only remains to ask at the shop for the types that are available to suit the job in hand.

To generalize, the trend is to make hinges for furniture in such form that they have either a round block base or a self aligning bracket for fixing. The round block form originated in the mass production furniture industry for two reasons. One, that particle board does not hold screws well and two, that machine bored socket holes are easily and accurately made. The hinge can then simply be plugged into the hole and either glued or screwed in. Assembly lines exist that feed the panels, bore the holes, inject glue, knock in the hinge and fix it with a screw, all without hand work.

The home handyman or woodworker must purchase a boring tool to use these hinges. The standard drill or bit with a long centre brad will not do; its centre point will penetrate and show through. The tool purchased with the plug hinges fits into the standard electric drill and bores a large round accurate hole to size and with a flat bottom. The tool has a surrounding-rim cutting edge to prevent side movement and so it can bore holes that actually break out through the edge of the cabinet end.

Hinges and hinge applications are shown in Figs. 37 and 38.

OTHER FITTINGS

Fasteners are again changing rapidly, both for joinery and furniture work. In a book of this type it is only possible to repeat the advice to seek help from a knowledgeable 'Home Handyman' storekeeper.

Accurate fitting is essential. Most fittings have at least two holes one of which is a slot, and a spur. The principle is that the slotted hole is for the purpose of temporary location until the correct register is obtained with the other part of the fastener. When accurately located a second screw is screwed into the round hole and this drives in the gripping spur that prevents slip.

To secure strong screw fixing into particle board, three methods are possible. The screw hole may be filled with glue before the screw is inserted. A dowel hole is bored and plugged with a glued dowel and the screw is inserted into the dowel, or special particle board screws may be used. These resemble standard screws but have parallel shanks, a coarse worm and no part of the shank that is not threaded. These give reasonable strength. The real answer is to spread the load by using large fittings and to insert screws carefully and avoid over turning.

Fig. 39 shows the methods of fitting butt hinges.

Fig. 37.
Hinge situations:
1 Standard butt hinge on solid or plywood.
2 Standard butt on solid or plywood.
3 Require special plug hinge (chipboard).
4 Another type of special chipboard hinge is required for 180° opening.
5 Rabbeted hinge for kitchen flap.
6 Surface fitting rabbeted hinge.
7 Special top and bottom pivots give 270° opening.
8 Rule-joint hinge for table flaps.
9 'Easy-Clean' casement pivot gives full clearance.
10 External doors and flaps use surface fitting 'T' type hinges.

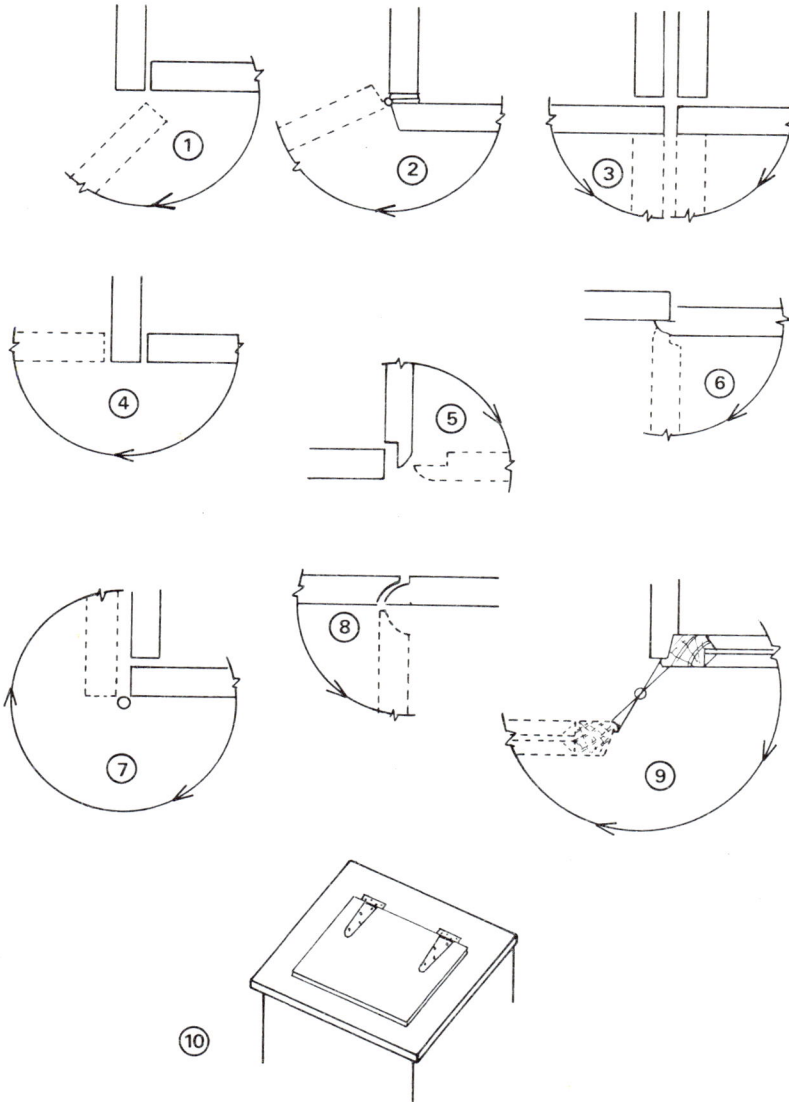

Fig. 38.
1 Butt hinge.
2 Back flap.
3 Rule-joint.
4 'Hurlinge' patent, requires no chopping in.
5 Special plug type hinge to give flush alignment through 90°.
6 Top and bottom pivots to give 270° of opening.
7 Rabbeted cabinet hinge.
8 'T' or Cross-Garnet hinge.
9 Plug cutter for electric drill. Required for modern plastic hinges for chipboard.

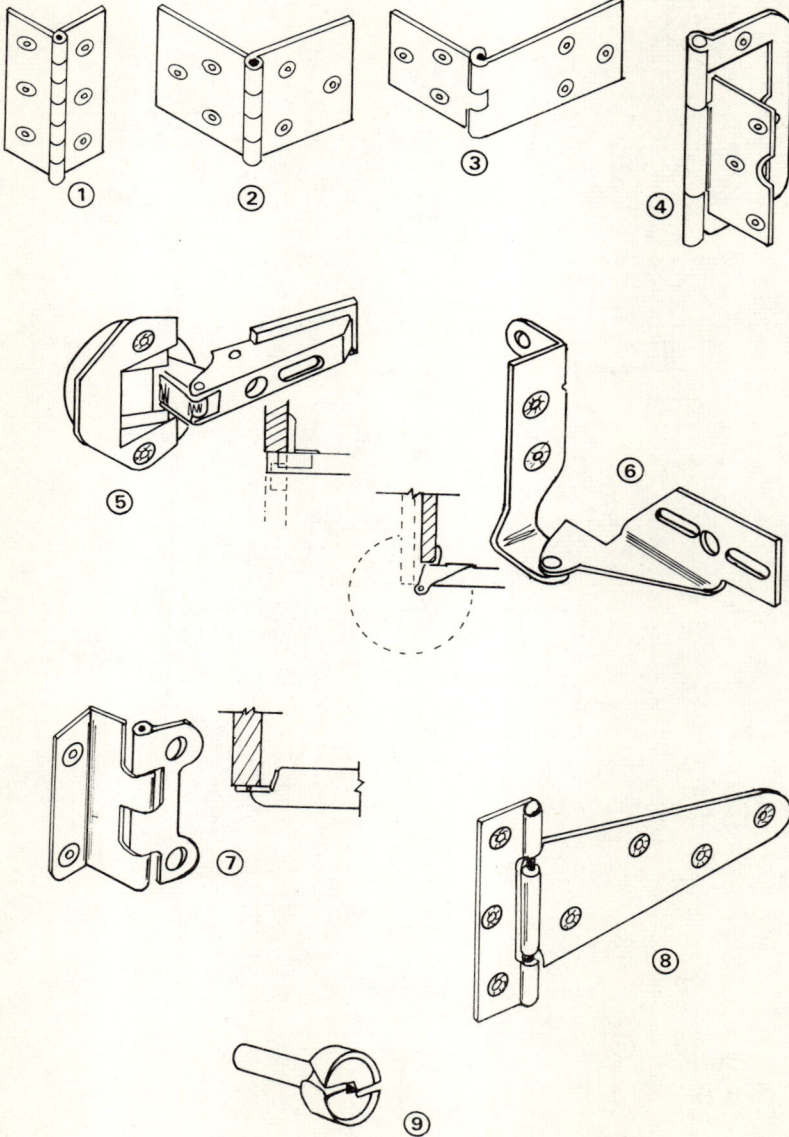

Fig. 39.
a To secure screws into chipboard: pre-bore and glue in dowel plug; or, use glue in hole as screw is inserted; or, use special parallel shank chipboard screws.
b b and b show the setting of two gauges for marking for brass and steel butt hinges.
c 1 to 5 show the stages of cutting-in butt hinges.
d Hinge positions for standard door.
e When hanging, screw only one screw into each plate of butt. Assist door location by driving heavy panel pins to bottom and back of cut slot.
To support door whilst planing its edge make up a support shoe.

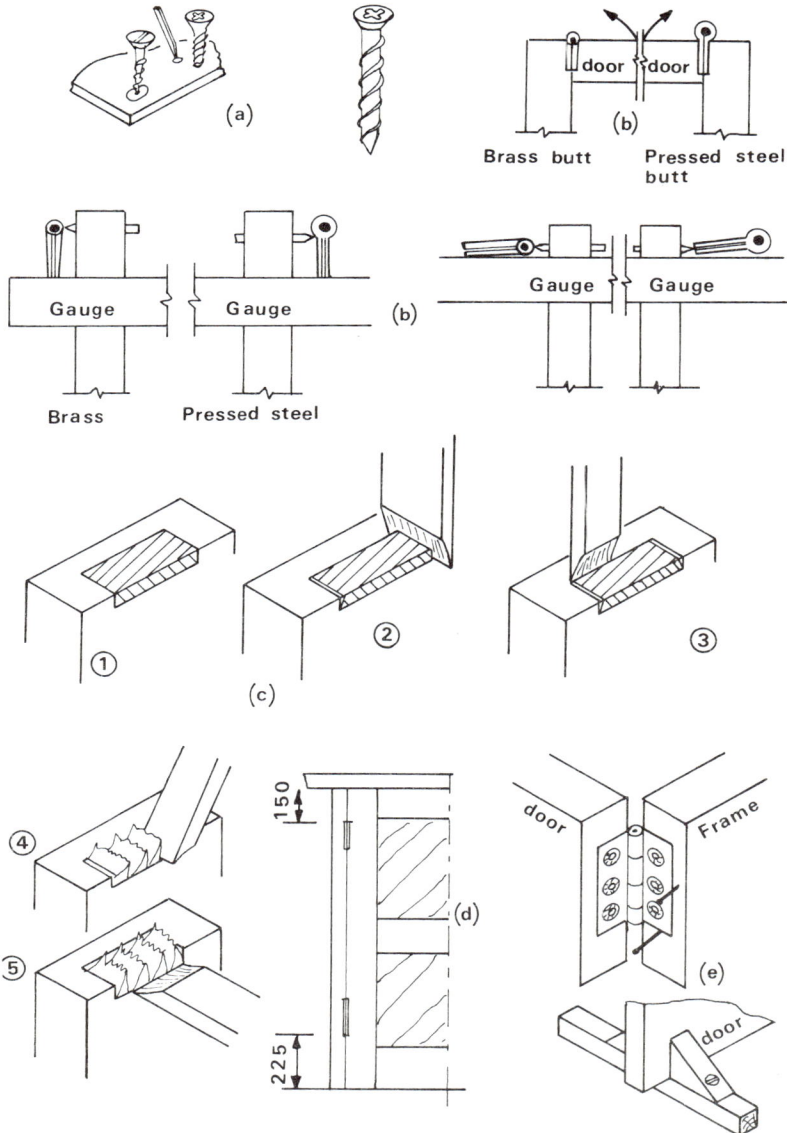

(a)

(b)

Brass butt   Pressed steel butt

Gauge   Gauge   (b)   Gauge   Gauge

Brass   Pressed steel

(c)

① ② ③

④ ⑤

150   (d)   225

door   Frame

(e)

door

109

Mention must be made of K.D. fittings. These are KNOCK DOWN fittings which are really knock-up fittings for they are fittings that may be used to build cabinet furniture from chipboard where traditional joints are not practical. They take many forms, but all have the same principle. This is that the two parts of the fitting are screwed to the two pieces that are to be joined. These are then offered together and a screw or key is inserted or turned in such a manner as to firmly lock the two parts of the fitting together. Very accurate positioning is essential and a trial run on spare pieces of board is advisable. These fittings do save an enormous amount of joint cutting and should be employed where their use is possible.

Wood is absorbent; it attracts and absorbs moisture. In doing so it swells and it may also, in a damp state, invite attack by fungus and insect. Having gained moisture during damp conditions, it will proceed to lose it during dry and warm spells. It then shrinks. As it shrinks it moves and will, maybe, twist and split.

Accordingly the finished job of woodwork must be protected by the application of a surface finish.

This surface finish may be entirely functional as with CREOSOTE, a coal-tar-based, dark brown wood preservative, or it may add additional eye appeal to the job and make for easy cleaning. In this class come paint, waxes and polishes. Surface finishes may also add protection from the hazards of use.

PAINTING

Paints are brushed or sprayed on, or applied by paint roller. The surface must be prepared to receive such paint. Assuming new wood, the process is as follows:

Apply KNOTTING, a shellac mixture that is not soluble in wood turpentine. The purpose of knotting is to prevent the finishing coat from being spoiled by natural wood oils creeping out as the wood dries. Knotting is painted over all knots on the raw wood, thus creating a non-dissolving barrier between the wood oils and the paint film.

Then PRIMING is applied. This has the purpose of filling and sealing the pores of the wood grain to prevent undue absorption of the following paint coats. Priming also offers a better key to the paint than the plain wood surface itself. Modern primers are complex and are usually lead-free. The early primers were based on lead, which had the ability of deep penetration and good drying, and resistance to attack by fungus, but these are now frowned upon because of the toxious nature of lead.

Two thin coats of primer are better than one thicker coat as this method allows greater penetration. For interior decorating one coat of emulsion paint is a reasonably efficient primer as it has good adhesion, quick drying, and good obliteration properties.

Following priming comes FILLING and STOPPING. Stopping is the process of filling the large holes caused by punched-in nail heads, loose knots and cracks and splits. Lead putty was favourite at one time but today the modern cellulose-based powdered fillers are most used. These are provided in packets and only require the addition of water. When mixed, the filler should be as thick in consistency as can be conveniently knifed in. All holes are treated, and the filler is knifed well in and struck off almost flush with the surface. When dry, the whole surface should be lightly sanded down, filled holes and primed wood. External grade fillers must be used for outdoor work.

Filling as distinct from stopping is the process of flowing a thin coat of filler fully out across the wood surface. This fills grain pin points and hair cracks that have been missed by stopping. It also fills sandpaper scratches. The home woodworker will only fill a surface if he requires a superlative finish. It requires skill and time and makes a lot of dust, for when dry, the filled area is sanded dead smooth, leaving no marks at all. Fine fillers are marketed by Polyfilla.

After the stopping process comes undercoating; for very light colours white emulsion paint may again be used.

Any undercoat used must have two main properties. It must flat out well and leave no brush marks, and it must have sufficient pigment solids to obliterate efficiently other colours that may tend to show through. Most modern p.v.a. emulsions have these properties and they have also very high adhesion. For top quality work an oil-based traditional undercoat is better than emulsion paint, for it flats better and has more body.

Once the undercoat is dry it should be given a very light 'finger touch' rub-down with fine abrasive paper. After dusting the job is ready for gloss or egg-shell finish.

Most modern paints require very little brushing out. The brush is dipped and squeezed on the side of the can to distribute the paint throughout the brush hair. The job is to brush out the paint and to leave a firm gloss surface with full coverage but with no brush marks.

The technique is to brush out over as large an area as the full brush will cover, then to cross by lighter and lighter brush strokes. The last touch should follow the longest direction of the work surface. However, with quick drying paints, over-brushing will spoil the gloss. Two thin coats are better than one thick coat.

Work Order

Most jobs should be started at the top and worked down. Panels in frames should be painted first, then horizontal rails, and finally the vertical members. A fairly quick way to gloss-paint large areas such as flush doors is to use a paint roller to apply a film and then to lay it all off by brushing. New hardboard should be painted with a watered emulsion paint to fill and seal its surface. When dry and rubbed down, use undercoat and gloss.

With all gloss paints it pays to work reasonably fast for, with quick drying, lap overs show easily. In this respect the most recent water-based soft gloss paints are most easily handled.

Fig. 40 shows the stages of surface finishing by liquid films.

112

Fig. 40.
a Stopping.
b Knife filling.
c Swab filling.
d 'Laying-off' gloss paint.
e Painting sequence.
f Staining: swab on—wipe off.
g Polishing: first fadding.

h Bodying.
i Spiriting off.
j Preparing rubber.
k Finished rubber.

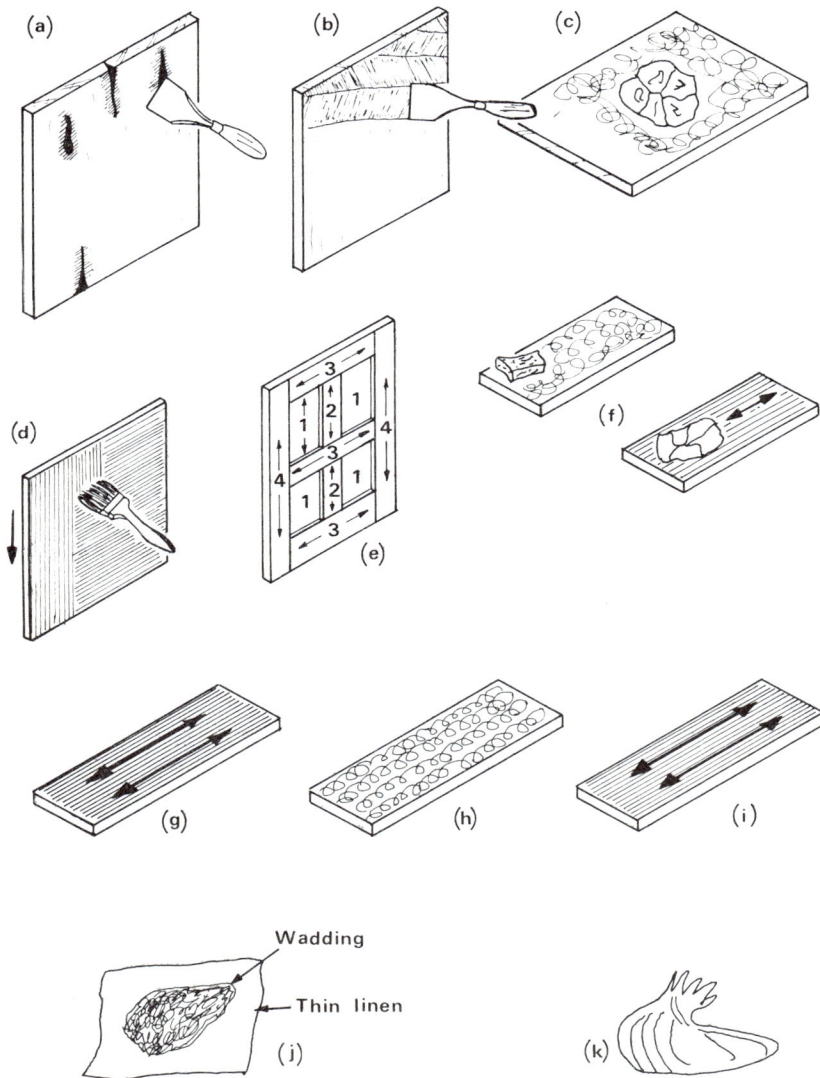

(a)

(b)

(c)

(d)

(e)

(f)

(g)

(h)

(i)

Wadding

Thin linen

(j)

(k)

VARNISHES

A varnish, as far as the user is concerned, is a transparent gloss or semi-gloss finish that enhances appearance by allowing the attractive wood grain to show. Like everything else in this chemical world, formulations change and the degree of glossiness and durability of varnishes varies with each compilation.

In general, varnishes should be brushed on from full brushes and allowed to flow. Over-brushing usually spoils the end result, for air bubbles are trapped, and very fine rough points are left in the dried coat.

To obtain a good finish the first coat should be flowed on, brushed out and allowed to dry. When hard dry the job should be rubbed down with very fine WET OR DRY abrasive paper. This paper is coated with silicon carbide, a very hard, sharp abrasive crystal which is bonded to the backing with a waterproof adhesive.

With fine touch control and a copious flow of water that has had a little detergent mixed with it the job is de-nibbed, which means that the fine mountanous peaks of dust, air bubbles and surface craters are rubbed flat. The shine goes dull but the surface will be flat. The next coat of varnish should be sparingly applied and brushed out in one direction. This will dry to full gloss. If an even better finish is required, a third coat is applied after another fine rub down.

Should a matt, or semi-gloss finish be required varnishes may be purchased that dry to give these non-gloss surfaces, but a better job results from the use of a hard, high-gloss varnish which has been cut down with wire wool and hard wax.

Varnishes may be one or two-pack if they are modern synthetics. They harden by chemical action as well as by loss of solvent. The one-pack cans have the hardener incorporated, but the two-pack types have a hardener to mix into the varnish before application. One-packs are not usually external material. The best externals are the two-pack yacht varnishes.

An attractive range of transparent wood finishes is marketed by the firm Izal Ltd., and is sold under the brand name of RONSEAL. These are polyurethane based and may be clear or coloured, glazed or mattcoat.

POLISHING

Polishing, as distinct from varnishing, is the process of developing a shine on wood surfaces in such a way as to make it appear that there has been no surface skin applied at all. A good polished job looks as though the wood itself is shining.

French polish is shellac dissolved in methylated spirit. The process of application is highly skilled but reasonable results are fairly easily achieved after a few trials. To start with, the polisher prepares a rubber. This is a mat of cotton wool that is wadded into a pear-shaped pad. Around this is a linen wrapper, pulled smooth and firm with its end twisted into a holding knob. The wood surface is prepared by sanding, staining and filling (reference to these processes later) and the polishing is begun by the application of a thin film of polish which is to act as a sealer.

Polishes are named as FRENCH, BUTTON, CLEAR, WHITE or GARNET. The most easy to use is button polish for it is slightly slower drying and is not so sticky as the others. It will however give a yellow tint to the job so it is not used on light coloured woods.

Polish is best kept in a bottle that has a small hole punched in its stopper or cap. A small amount of polish is poured through this hole on to the pad to charge the rubber.

With light, regular strokes, the rubber is moved in straight lines end to end of the work leaving a thin skin of polish in its wake. Slight overlap will ensure that the polish is laid wet on wet. When this first coat is finished the surface will be sealed. Pressure on the rubber is light when fully charged, but must increase as the polish needs to be squeezed out.

Carrying on the process the polisher now charges his rubber with slightly more polish and works on circular sweeps across and along the surface. Very occasionally a few drips of linseed oil are dropped on the surface to lubricate the rubber. As work progresses the surface should begin to shine. When the skin appears sufficient it must be left to harden, at least overnight, but preferably longer. This process is called BODYING.

When hard and dry very light sanding is given using the finest, worn-out, old piece of sanding paper available, with a few drops of linseed oil as a lubricant. Hardly any pressure is needed.

The surface now will be flat and it will have a dull shine. The rubber is now charged with polish that has had a very small amount of methylated spirit added to it. This stage is called SPIRITING OFF, for the spirit serves the final purpose of achieving a high shine.

The diluted polish is thinner and flows more easily; the body coating has its top surface slightly softened, and the spirit also washes away the remnants of any excess of linseed oil. Very little polish is needed, for after a few straight line rubs, the shine should be apparant.

At all stages the rubber should start wet but appear dry at the end of the process. The last rubs of the spiriting off stage almost fulfill a burnishing function.

STAINING
Staining is the artificial colouring of wood in a way that allows the wood

grain to show through. Stains are based on many chemicals but the home woodworker only needs to buy ready-mixed tins of proprietary brands because these are most easily applied with few problems. Such stains are called SOLVENT-BASED stains, and have no water in them. Water stains tend to raise the wood grain. Solvent stains have good penetration and colour fastness although each job must be tested for colour before the main stain is applied. Stains are often called WOOD DYES and this is a good indication that you are dealing with a solvent stain rather than a water or naptha stain.

In general, all stains are applied with a coarse swab, hard sponge, or brush. The swab method is most simple using a well-loaded swab across and along the grain. A dry swab is then used to wipe off all surplus. Corners that will collect heavy deposits of stain must be well dried to avoid dark appearance. When fully dry—overnight—rub surface with a clean dry rag before any further treatment. Chipboard should be sealed before staining, for it is particularly absorbent and tends to go patchy and to give a much darker effect than that required by choice of stain.

A very good range of wood dyes is marketed under the label COLRON Wood Dye as part of the RONCRAFT system by Izal Ltd.

SURFACE PREPARATION
When the project has been glued and cleaned-up, using cutting tools such as the smoothing plane, it must be SANDED. 'Sanding' is a misnomer, since no sand is used today. The tool used for smoothing is, in general, called sand-paper, but it is in fact a tool that has many variations. The correct description is COATED ABRASIVES. These are sheets of special paper coated with grits of special nature. In use, the many thousands of sharp points each act as cutting agents and according to the size of the particles they smooth to a more or less degree.

The abrasive crystals used for handwork are now silica (glass), or garnet, a natural mined stone that has been heat-treated to increase hardness and sharpness. The silica is bottle glass processed into graded size particles. Garnet is very hard and sharp and gives much the best performance. The two grits are evenly strewn across the backing paper and bonded thereon by glueing.

Glass-paper is yellow in appearance but in its very fine grades, called FLOUR PAPER it goes to a pale grey/green. Garnet is red/brown, and is very much more costly but does far more work.

Grading for commercial purposes is by a number code—each code figure being the size of hole in the sieve, or screen by which the particles have been size sorted. A code of 180 grit indicates that the screen mesh has holes measuring 1/180 in. × 1/180 in. This would be fine paper. Sand-paper so called (but more correctly glass-paper), has its own arbitary grade code. This code starts at 00 or Flour, and runs through to No. 3. Garnet starts at 10/0 (another arbitary code), screen size 400 and goes up to No. $3\frac{1}{2}$, screen size 20.

For home use middle range papers are used. For softwoods taken flat by plane an M2 (middle 2) glass-paper or garnet grade $\frac{1}{2}$ (60) is used to give preliminary smoothness, to be followed by either grade 1 or $1\frac{1}{2}$ glass-paper or garnet grade 2/0 or 3/0 (130). This will leave a painting-smooth surface. For rougher work, start with an S2 glass paper (sharp 2) or garnet 1 (50) and finish with glass-paper 0 or garnet 4/0 (150).

Hardwood must be treated carefully, for scratches are difficult to eradicate. Progressive use of finer abrasives is the answer.

Paper first with small circular motion using paper wrapped around a cork block. Finishing strokes should be in-line with the grain.

CUTTING BACK
Cutting back is the process of de-nibbing (smoothing) polishes or paints between first coats and top coats. The abrasives used for this are flour glass paper, 7/0 (240 garnet) or Wet and Dry Silicon Carbide. The first two are not very effective for they clog easily. The Wet and Dry is waterproof, with a very sharp and even abrasive. It is dull black in colour. Use water and detergent and rub with finger pressure over a small area at a time. Use paper from 220 to 320 grit.

SURFACING WITH SHEET MATERIALS
These are rigid laminated plastics, flexible plastic films and wood veneers.

Rigid plastics are an ideal surface, reasonably permanent and easily handled. They may be cut to size by woodworking saws and planed or filed to produce smooth edges.

The technique is to cut slightly over-size, say about 3 mm overhang, but this depends on the skill available. Using contact adhesive both plastic and substrate (the job) are evenly coated and screeded (even rippled surface) and left for about 15/20 minutes for adhesive solvent to evaporate. When touch dry the two surfaces are closed. This is where the skill comes in, for once positioned, movement to any degree is not possible. Use drawing pins as a guide or stop, and press firmly down from centre outwards. When using the thixotropic variety of adhesive some slide is possible until full pressure is exerted. Where a bench vice is available the edge of any panel may be squeezed for extra pressure, working all round. Both sides of thin panels must be treated using the cheapest form of laminated plastic for the back surface. This prevents bowing due to uneven tensions. Chipboard of 18 mm stays reasonably flat with only one face surfaced.

Wood Veneers

Wood veneers are expensive to buy. Mostly they can only be bought in leaf form. A leaf is one slice of veneer from a bundle cut from one board in the veneer mill. It follows that, unless trimmed and clipped, the leaf will follow the shape of the board from which it is cut and contain all surface imperfections such as knots and sapwood. Furniture firms overcome this by selective cutting, using the best pieces for fronts and the second best for ends. Anything else is used for inside drawers and shelves etc.

However, there are veneers made up into a range of panel strips for the home woodworker. These are mostly teak type and mahogany type (type, because there are so many similar appearing timbers, some of which are cheaper than others, and some of which are more easily cut into veneer) and these are cut very thin and then two are glued face to face to make a veneer suitable for home application.

Traditionally, hand veneering is an animal glue process. Commercially, veneers are laid by press, using synthetic adhesives. To veneer by hand the substrate is made flat and if possible, TOOTHED. This means that it has its surface roughened with a plane-like tool having a cutter with a serrated edge. It is not essential however.

The veneer is cut to approximate size and various pieces are matched for appearance.

Then the substrate is coated with SIZE, which is scotch glue slightly diluted with water, and used very hot. When this is dry, veneering is commenced. The tools used are: A glue pot with clean, hot, fluid scotch glue, a brush, a hot flat iron (electric or gas heated), rag swabs, hot water and a veneer hammer, which is simply a tool having a rounded pressure edge about 100 mm long. A trimming knife is also required.

Both veneer and the substrate are given a thin coat of hot glue. The veneer is then placed on the substrate and pressed home with the edge of the veneer hammer, working with zig-zag motion from centre out to the edges.

The object is to squeeze out as much glue as possible (there will always be enough left) and to leave no trapped thick pockets. To prevent curl-up of veneer the top surface is washed over with hot water. As the glue jells it is reheated with the hot iron. *If this is electric it must not be plugged in whilst working.* A wet rag is placed between veneer and the sole of the iron. As the glue melts it is squeezed out once more. When the first piece is firmly down, the next is treated, lapping over the first piece at the jointing edge. This piece too is hammered down.

118

Fig. 41.

a Use drawing pins, or tack on guides when applying laminate.
b Chamfer edges of laminates.
c Pre-coated edge veneers are laid with hot iron and then pressed down.

d Laminates may be pressed down at edges in the bench vice. Edging strips may be pressed on with 3-way edge cramps.

(continued on following page)

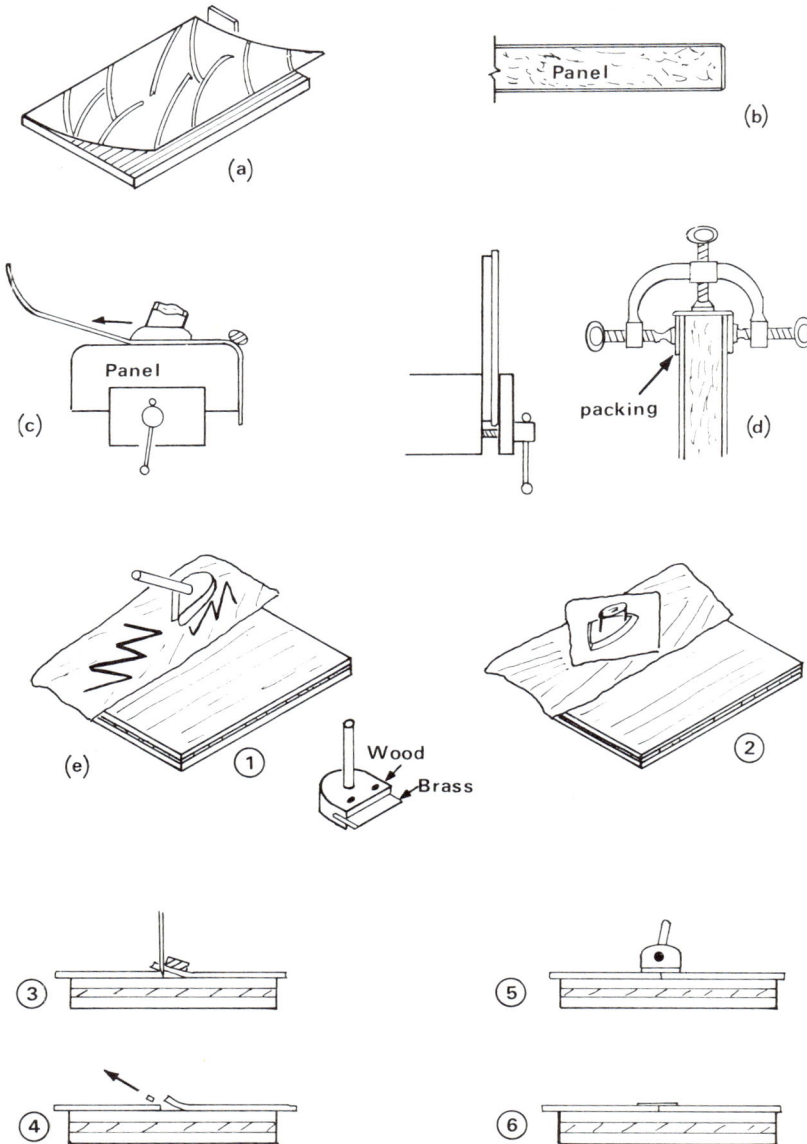

(a)

Panel

(b)

Panel

(c)

packing

(d)

(e)

①

Wood
Brass

②

③

④

⑤

⑥

e Veneering stages:
1 Coat panel and veneer with glue and press down.
2 Re-heat with iron. ·
3 To make join, cut with knife along straight edge.
4 Peel up and lift away waste.
5 Re-heat and press firmly down with veneer hammer.
6 Paper tape the joint to hold edges together.

To make the joint, a steel rule is positioned over the lapped edges, and the knife is used to cut through both thicknesses of veneer. The top waste is peeled off and discarded. Then the iron is used to melt the glue beneath the joint. One edge is lifted and the second piece of waste is peeled off and discarded. Then the two edges are pressed once more with the hammer. When the joint is closed it is TAPED, the process of sticking a piece of paper along it to hold it whilst the glue sets.

A final wash with the swab and the job is left to dry. When dry it is sanded and the edges are trimmed.

EDGE FINISHING

Edges of all panels faced with plastics or wood veneers should be protected. This may be done by edge veneering, after having cut narrow veneer strips, using the same veneering technique.

A point to remember is that with modern thixotropic adhesives, small jobs may be wood veneered without the mess of wet glueing. Both surfaces are coated, allowed to dry, and pressed home with the veneer hammer. Edges may be treated in like manner.

Yet another way is to purchase pre-glued edge strip veneer. These are coated with HOTMELT glue. This is a modern industrial glue that changes from solid to fluid and back with only slight change in temperature. It has no solvent to lose. Thus if the edge strip is positioned, it may be ironed on with a hot iron and pressed home with a wood block.

Melamine (hard plastic) edging strip may also be bought coated with 'Hot Melt' but it is very thin and is best used for curved work only.

Better protection is given if hard plastic laminate is used for edging. The strip is cut over width, coated with contact adhesive and applied to the squared up panel edge. Surplus is planed down and then filed flush, finishing with a slight bevel to protect the faces of the top and edge laminates.

Fig. 41 indicates methods of surfacing with the use of laminates and veneers.

12 Timber in the House

Before alterations, repairs and additions to the house are made, it is necessary to know the purpose for which each piece of timber is positioned and the reason for such positioning.

In general, timber in the traditional house starts below floor level and rises, with the construction, through to the highest part of the roof, the ridge.

Each has its part to play and if the householder knows what this part is, he may with greater safety cut and displace.

Modern houses may vary in that they have no ground floor timber or have framed plywood walls with external brick cladding, but generally the use of timber has only changed in quantity and dimension.

FLOORS AND MATERIALS

Ground floors of planed, square edged boards—P.A.R. FLOORING—planed, all round flooring, are supported on floor joists. These are heavy section sawn timber, called constructional timber, not because it has been selected for construction but because it has been rejected for JOINERY timber, which is the clean, knot-free material able to take joints and to machine cleanly to section. Constructional timber is sometimes called CARCASING and under this name you will expect to buy a rough low grade sawn material either of DOUGLAS FIR or REDWOOD.

These timbers, and others, are described later in Chapter 14.

To return to floors. The joists are built-in on edge and may be as deep as 175 mm but with modern houses they are usually either 100 mm or 125 mm in depth by 63 mm or 75 mm in sawn thickness. Older houses have more excess of timber and so more may be cut away or altered without fear. Spacing of the joists depends on the type of floor boarding and is easily seen from the nail spacings of strip floors. Nails must be kept to the edges of the floor boards because some previous occupier may have notched an electric cable or gas pipe into the joist tops.

The direction of the joists is opposite to the run of the floor boards, so if one board is taken up all the joists are seen. Pipes or cables are easily threaded between joists or below them, but if they must follow the run of the floor boards then each joist must be bored to take them (unless the floor is suspended sufficiently for them to go underneath). It is not good practice to notch the tops of floor joists because of the risk from flooring nails.

The ends of the joists are supported on dwarf walls built on the site concrete. Firstly, a slate or bituminous D.P.C. (damp-proof course) is laid and the joists are positioned on this and levelled. Older houses will have a timber wall-plate along the top of the dwarf wall. The joists rest on this. A honeycombed dwarf wall is built across the room centre to support centres of the joists. Usually joists span the short length of the room. The honeycombed brick wall makes it possible to thread cables and pipes across below a floor, searching out the holes with sweep rods or fishing rods. Below the level of the floor there are air bricks set in the walls to ventilate the underfloor space. These must never be closed or dry rot may then grow. Where fireplaces are, the joists are trimmed into a crossing joist, called the TRIMMER. Usually there is a space between this trimmer and the concrete hearth, thus making it easy to thread cable for power points. Joists parallel to walls have spacers between them and the walls, and this again is useful for re-wiring jobs. Fig. 42 shows the arrangement of a typical ground floor.

First Floors

These are suspended floors and the joists are kept as short as possible and are deeper in section. Between them to keep them stiff and steady there are herring-bone struts. These make it slightly more difficult to thread cable along the joist length, but again, a rod used as a probe may carry the first cable end along.

First floor joists may be supported on built-in metal hangers or on projecting bricks. On older houses they may be built into the wall. The joist closest to the wall will be packed away to leave a space. If it is necessary to lay a cable across an upstairs floor it is best to bore through the joists using a 16/18 mm bit and boring at an angle downwards, keeping to the top third of the joists and keeping central to the floor boards. Some floor boards run under a dividing wall on upper floors where these have been built after the floor has been laid. Such walls are usually of breeze block or are stud partitions (timber). To lift such boards it is necessary to bore a 12 mm hole close to the skirting and close to the board edge. Then use a padsaw to cut across. To re-lay such a board, a cross piece should be screwed across on the underside of the floor boards. Fig. 43 gives upper floor details.

Ceilings

Ceiling joists vary according to span but on average are about 50 mm × 100 mm. They are supported at their ends on wall plates. They carry the weight of the ceiling plaster board. Loft tanks should be positioned over the walls and not carried on the joists. Each joist will have nailed to it the end of a rafter, which is the sloping timber that meets the house wall with its lower end, and supports the central horizontal ridge at its top end. To stiffen the rafter, purlins run along their undersides. The purlins are supported by struts that go down to the ceiling joists.

Old houses have excessive timber, and some struts may be moved to provide more space in a loft. Modern roofs that have thin boards used on

Fig. 42.
a This figure shows typical cross-section along a ground floor.
b This shows the same construction, but across the room and includes the honeycomb dwarf wall for ventilation.
c Floors are trimmed round the fireplace concrete.

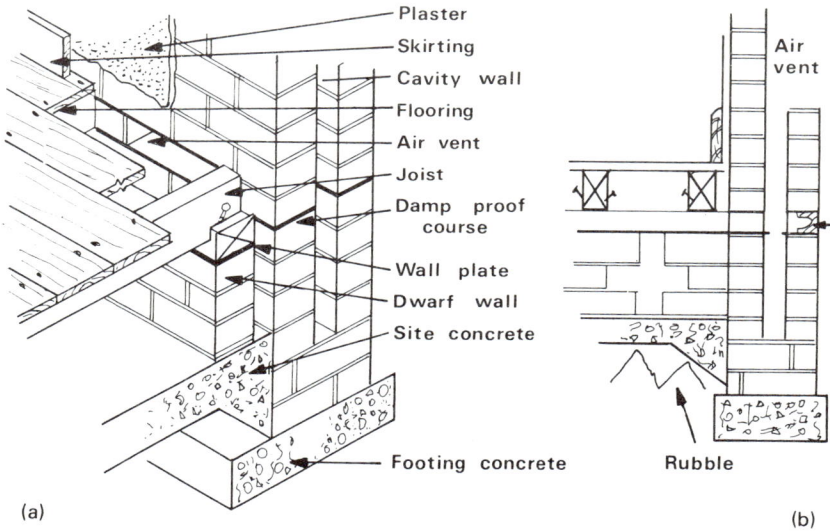

— Plaster
— Skirting
— Cavity wall
— Flooring
— Air vent
— Joist
— Damp proof course
— Wall plate
— Dwarf wall
— Site concrete
— Footing concrete

(a)

Air vent

Rubble

(b)

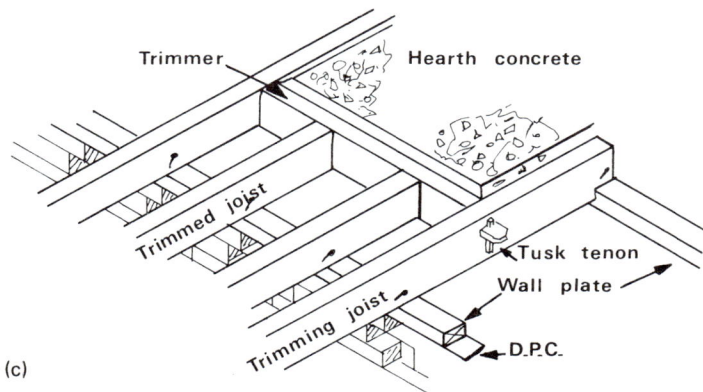

Trimmer   Hearth concrete

Trimmed joist

Trimming joist

Tusk tenon
Wall plate
D.P.C.

(c)

Fig. 43.

a Upper floor construction.

b Herring-bone strutting to stiffen joists.

c Bore holes through top part of joist to thread under-floor cable.

d To cut a trap first bore hole and then use toe of tenon saw. Screw block to joist to re-lay trap.

e To raise a centre board spring up with a bolster chisel and wedge, then cut at joist centre.

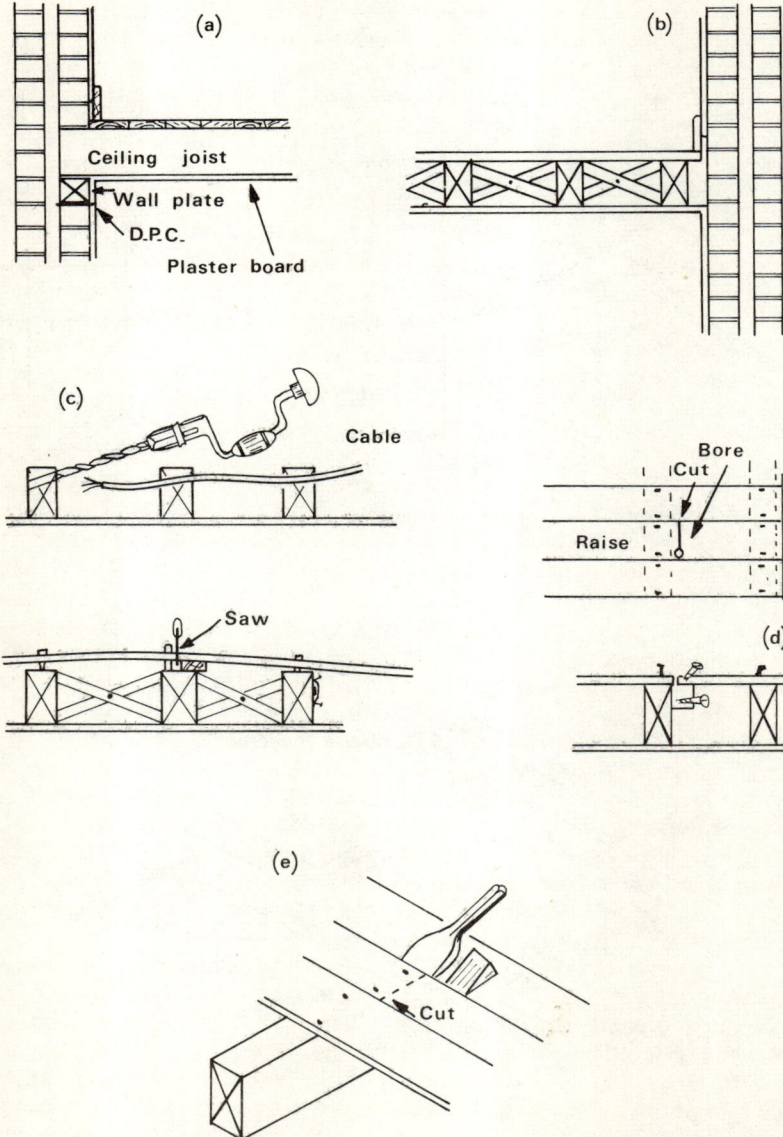

(a)

Ceiling joist

Wall plate

D.P.C.

Plaster board

(b)

(c)

Cable

Saw

Bore

Cut

Raise

(d)

(e)

Cut

edge to form trusses, have no spare material, neither have roofs with solid timber trusses. Trusses are triangular self-supporting frames on which all rafters are supported by purlins. All alterations to roofs must be checked with a good builder, for some members carry compressive loads and some tensile loads and a cut tie or prop could disturb the roof strength.

THE JOINERY AND TRIM

JOINERY is the cupboards, doors, door-frames, windows, window frames and stairs. TRIM is the skirting, architrave and picture rails.

Door frames have jambs; the verticals, and a head, the top horizontal. The head usually has horns that project beyond the jambs. These are built-in and a plaster skin conceals them. They form a convenient position for cable holes for telephone, door bells and extension speakers. Heads are mortise and tenoned to jambs and then spiked with 100 mm nails, which make it difficult to bore through in-line with the jambs. Frames are fixed to walls by screws into wood plugs or breeze fixing blocks. When the frames are fixed as the walls are built they may have galvanised anchor brackets screwed on, and these are mortared into the course work of the bricks. External frames have a short steel rod inserted into the foot of each jamb and this goes into the floor unless there is a timber threshold, when the jambs are tenoned into this. Window frames are fixed in the same manner but without the steel rods.

SKIRTINGS, the protection given to the wall at its junction with the floor, are usually fixed after the wall has been plastered. The FIRST FIXER, the carpenter who makes ready all the plugs and grounds required for SECOND FIXING, the job of fitting units and cabinets etc. fixes grounds into the brickwork. These are vertical for skirtings and are called SOLDIERS. They are themselves nailed to plugs in the wall. The skirting is nailed to the grounds and so, for cable and conduit alterations it is possible to plough the plaster down to the skirting line and then to knock down behind the skirting until the end of the rod used for tracking is felt under the floor. The floor board may have to be holed here if it extends too far beyond the skirting. The plaster does not go down to the floor but stops just below the top line of the skirting. See Fig. 44.

If a new piece of skirting has to be fitted the soldiers must be lined up by packing and the lower edge of the skirting be scribed to the floor. To do this the skirting length is raised on blocks of about 12 mm and adjusted until its top edge is level. Dividers are then set to the greatest gap between floor and lower edge of skirting. With one leg on the floor the dividers are drawn along and the top leg scribes the skirting. This gives a mark for planing.

Picture rails are nailed to plugs or directly into breeze-block walls, and

Fig. 44.
a Plug socket boxes should be 305 mm
from the floor. Cut cavity into plaster and
brick; run down channel for conduit,
breaking through behind skirting as at b.
c Fixing positions for ceiling fittings
must be in-line with joists. Use fine probe
to locate joist.

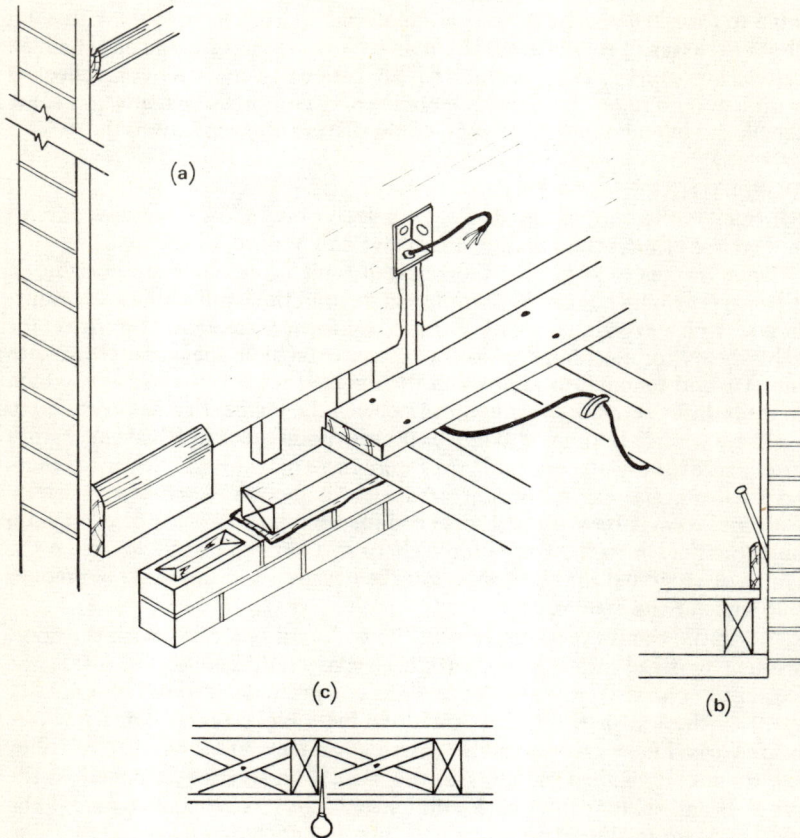

(a)

(c)

(b)

they must be set horizontal, otherwise patterned paper will not hang very
well. The ARCHITRAVE is the trim around door and window frames.
Depending on the type of frame, solid or framed-up, the architrave will be
nailed directly into the solid frame, or into the frame grounds if the frame is
framed-up. Sometimes, where framed-up door frames are fitted there is a
cavity between the wall, the ground, and the edge of the frame, and this
cavity is covered by the architrave. Removal of the architrave will allow
such a cavity to be used for cable running.

Stair-treads are solid and are housed into the STRINGS which are the
wide side members of a staircase. The treads and risers are wedged into

these housings on manufacture. After years of use the treads shrink and the wedges come loose. This is one reason for the annoying stair creak often heard. Access under the stairs is usually through the SPANDREL panelling at the side. This can be removed to make an open space for the telephone etc., as it carries no load. The heavy NEWEL (stair post) must not be touched. To return to the creaking stair. Once under the stair it is possible to prize out the wedges and to cut and glue in new ones. It is hot, dirty work but it does help to lose the creak.

FITMENTS
Built-in cupboards of early design are usually plywood and frame construction, panelled up and nailed to floor and skirtings with the top rails sometimes nailed back to wall. Mostly they will have a false floor and this again will allow quick running of cable from room to room by drilling right through skirting, wall, and skirting.

PARTITIONS
A partition, in building terms, is a light weight wall that carries no weight. Some of these are of breeze block construction but the carpenter is not concerned with this type.

Timber partitions are called STUD partitions because the vertical members are called studs.

Where it is necessary to divide a room a stud partition is fairly easily erected. The material used is sawn 75 mm × 50 mm carcassing. The only joints are half-laps, housings and notchings, although mortise and tenons should be used for the four corners. The floor piece, called the PLATE, or cill, is nailed to the floor. It should go across the joists or be in-line with one joist. A ceiling piece, called the HEAD, is notched on to the top ends of the studs. The spacing of the studs should be such that they allow the facing board, either building board, plasterboard or hardboard, to be nailed on all edges. Standard plaster board is called GYPSUM WALL BOARD and consists of a sandwich of plaster between two paper skins, with the paper of one face wrapped round the two long edges. One side has an ivory coloured paper and the other, a grey one. The grey side has a double thickness of paper along each edge. The ivory side is the side to face out for home decoration purposes, for the other side is intended to take skim coats of plaster, and this is hardly within the sphere of the home carpenter. The ivory side is sometimes bevelled on edge or slightly tapered. This allows a joint filler to be used to conceal the joint, and the tapered edge allows for a building tape to be stuck along the joint to bring it flush in appearance. The board is fixed with galvanised steel nails, punched home and filled.

To return to the studding; the board sizes are standard at 9·5 mm ($\frac{3}{8}$ in.) thick by 600, 900, and 1200 mm wide. In length they go from 1800, 2400 to 3000 mm. Availability should be checked before building the studding.

Having fixed the plate, head and studs, NOGGINGS are fitted. These are horizontal stiffeners between studs. They are usually cut square to butt between studs, but may alternatively be fitted zig-zag, to allow nailing, for noggings are nailed by nails going through the studs and into the ends of the noggings.

Having assembled the partition, which should be shorter in height than the room, and shorter in length than the width of the room so that it may be erected more easily, grounds, or packing pieces, are fitted between ceiling and head and between walls and end studs.

When measuring, allowance must be made for any room skirting, picture rails or cornices. The noggings will also be lined up to allow for the fittings of picture rails and for two edges of adjacent boards to meet on them.

The noggings are smoothed down flush with the studs and the plaster board or other cladding is fitted. Nails are punched in, joints filled and taped and the picture rail and skirting are fitted.

To finish the partition at the corners and at the ceiling, scribing pieces are fitted, these are either quadrant beads, or small sections about 45 mm × 12 mm with one corner rounded. They cover the gap between studs and walls.

A lining paper is then hung and the wall has become a permanent fixture. Door openings are provided as the partition grows. A door TRANSOME, the horizontal rail above a door, is mortised and tenoned into the two studs which border the door opening. If the door is a light one then the transome may become the door frame head and the studs become the frame jambs. They will then need to be planed before assembly and be wider than the rest of the studding to make a stop for the plaster board. Otherwise a complete frame is screwed into the opening provided. After the boarding is fitted the door frame is finished with the addition of an architrave surround.

FLUSH DOORS

To convert a four panel door into a flush door, hardboard is used. One method is to purchase a small rabbeted beading with which to edge the hardboard, and the other is to take the hardboard as close as is possible to the door stops on the closing side of the door leaving a narrow margin, and completing flushing to the door edges on the opening side. Both arrangements are suitable. The edge mouldings must be mitred at their corners.

The panels are cut to size, or bought as door flushing panels ready cut, and they must be conditioned. This entails finding a flat floor where they may be laid overnight. Then the rough sides of the panels are washed over with a very wet cloth and the loose water swabbed away. They are then placed back to back (water to water) and left flat overnight. This swells the board material so that when it finally dries out it shrinks close to the door without bowing out.

Meanwhile the door is treated. Paint is heavily sanded down to give a flat surface. Some carpenters prefer to cut grooves across the rails about 4 mm × 4 mm so that when the panels are fitted there is always air behind them. This is debatable and has the disadvantage that the door is spoilt if fashion dictates a return to panelled doors.

The panels are fitted with hardboard pins, usually square-cut coppered nails that lose their heads in the boards. The trim moulding is fitted with fine panel pins. All visible holes are filled and a wash coat of watered emulsion paint is given as a sealer. If the edges of the hardboard are exposed then a watery Polyfilla solution is rubbed in with a finger to fill and seal such edges. If the beaded method is chosen the panel size must allow clearance for door furniture (knobs and finger plates etc.). With full surface flushing the furniture is removed and refixed after painting (as should always be done when decorating).

13 Electric Tools: Simple and Safe

Electric-powered hand tools are safe if used correctly, and have built-in safety factors even if they are sometimes perhaps, not used as correctly as they should be. The risk of injury from the cutting tools (saws, drills and sander discs) is probably higher than the risk of electrical injury.

Given correct wiring, regular servicing and reasonable use these tools should be as trouble-free in use as are chisels and planes.

MOTORS

Most home-use power tools employ the drill unit as the power pack. This limits the facility of use because of the need to switch the power-pack from accessory to accessory as different operations are required. Industrial power tools are specialist and require only to be set, or arranged, for the job they have to do. Because of this the home-use range is expanding all the time, and more and more single purpose power tools are being included in the range available.

The drill power-pack has a basic motor unit and then additionally, a gear box. The single speed drills are falling out of favour and to cater for the widest job range, modern drills have at least two speeds, either switched electrically or changed mechanically.

Many drills have two-speed switching and a two-speed mechanical gear box, making four speeds available. Use of the electrical thyristor now enables drills to be made with infinitely variable speed control by trigger pressure. Finally, the drill may have all of the above refinements plus a HAMMER BLOW setting. This setting will give a percussion impact to the drill point when a carbide tipped drill is being used to drill masonry and concrete. Drills need speed variation to adjust them to varying diameters of cutting tools.

Briefly, the motors are known as SERIES WOUND-UNIVERSAL motors. This means that they may be run on alternating or direct current—and if from alternating current, from 25Hz to 60Hz. This may appear 'double-dutch' to a non-electrical man, but it means that if the tool is used on British mains of 240 volts at 50 Hz (cycles per second) it will give maximum service. The trend is to wind them for a.c. only as this gives a smaller motor for the same power output.

Motors of this type—series wound—must have BRUSHES and COMMUTATORS. The first are small carbon blocks that carry the electric current from the stationary part of the tool to the moving part. The commutator is the segmented copper ring on which the brush rides and to which it, the brush, conducts electricity.

With a modern drill it is only the brushes and commutators that require servicing, and this only very occasionally. Excessive heat and yellow sparks seen through the air vents will indicate the need for servicing. The newer drills will be almost totally enclosed, and the commutator ring will not be visible, so heat will be the only indication of poor running. With bearings packed for life no lubrication is required for most drills. The only other service requirement is that of cable inspection. Cables should be inspected frequently for cracks in the wall, and at both ends, to see whether the cable is firmly anchored at plug and drill.

The note INTERMITTENT RATING sometimes included on the drill plate, simply means that the most efficient running temperature of the drill is achieved after a set period of running and thereafter normal usage—i.e., 'off' and 'on', will not harm the drill. It does mean however that a drill marked 'Intermittent' should not be fixed to a stand and left running for long periods. It would in fact cope with this because most power tools are over-rated in any case, but it could lead to eventual insulation breakdown.

Wiring
Older drills will have three wires, one red, one black and one green. Some will have the international wire colours of brown, pale blue and green/yellow.

The red, or brown, is the live lead and this must go to the terminal marked 'L' on the plug top. The black, or pale blue is the neutral lead and it must go to the terminal marked 'N'. The green/yellow lead is the earth protection wire and should go to the terminal marked 'E'.

Simply, this means that the live lead picks up the power supply from the live feed in the socket, feeds it through the fuse in the plug top and then feeds it along to the switch in the drill. When the switch is closed the live lead continues through to one brush. The power supply then rotates the ARMATURE (the rotating part) and is connected through the second brush to the return run (the neutral) directly back to the neutral line at the socket. The green or green/yellow line is connected at the socket back to an efficient and tested EARTH, which is merely a very good connection to the ground. When all is in order the 'earth' serves no purpose. Should a metallic part of the drill make contact with the 'live' then the earth immediately connects the power supply directly to ground. The sudden, and instanteous, flow of current is too great for the fuse and it blows, thereby breaking the circuit and all is safe.

So—for a three-wire drill the fuse must not be greater than the circuit requires. The drill will have its WATTAGE marked as 325 watt, 330 watt, 400 watt, and so on. The higher the wattage the greater the power output of the drill.

The equation is that $I = W/V$. Where I = amps, W = watts and V =

volts. All of which are marked on the drill. Simply divide the watts by the volts and this will give the fuse rating in amps.

Thus a drill marked 400 watts at 240 volts will give 400 over 240 = 1·6 approximately. Now this is unreasonable because the drill will take more power under load and at starting, so for absolutely safety, a 3 amp fuse should be fitted. For commonsense working all home power tools of less than 1200 watts (about $1\frac{1}{2}$ horse power) will be adequately protected by a 5 amp fuse.

Double Insulation

Almost every home-use power tool today is DOUBLE INSULATED. This means what it says. The internal electrical components are encapsulated within a covering non-conductive shield of plastic. The external case of the tool is made of a tough, shock (impact) resisting plastic. There can be no electrical path between the external metallic parts of the tool (the chucks, guards and accessories etc.) and the internal electrical bits and pieces.

In this situation the third, the earth wire, is no longer required or even desirable, and the tool can safely be run from a lighting, two point socket—provided that the lighting circuit is in good condition and has no higher fuse than 5 amp.

The wires will be blue and brown with the brown lead as the 'live'. The live lead should always be the one to connect to the switch in the tool and to the 'L' terminal in the plug top. 'Double Insulated' tools are marked with the 'Double Insulation' symbol, which consists of one small square inside another.

Fig. 45 shows details of wiring circuits of electric home use tools.

THE SAW UNIT

To use the power pack for sawing the drill chuck is removed—normally by knocking the spanner provided in the same direction as the chuck rotates. Some older drills have a tapered engineering 'grip' but most today have screw-in fittings.

The saw guard is fitted to the exposed spindle nose and the saw is fitted to this. Usually a small washer acts as a saw collar, and either a nut holds the saw and guard in place, or a threaded bolt enters the internal thread of the power-pack nose. The saw, guard and power-pack are then fitted to the sawing accessory. Details of these vary from make to make, but assembly instructions, easy to follow, come with the tool. It is rarely possible to switch accessories from one make of electric drill to another.

Saw size varies from 100 mm to 150 mm and this relates to the speed and power of the power-pack unit. Cutting depth with a circular saw of 150 mm

Fig. 45.

a This is the basic circuit for an a.c./d.c. power tool motor. In practice there would be more than two coils.

b Three wires are required for older electric tools: Live, Neutral, and Earth.

c Older tools use Red, Black, Green colour code; but now all new tools have Brown, Blue, Green/Yellow.

d Plug top connections: Brown to 'L'. Blue to 'N' and Green/Yellow to 'E'. Double squares on a tool indicate 'Double Insulation' and only two wires are required—Brown and Blue.

(continued on following page)

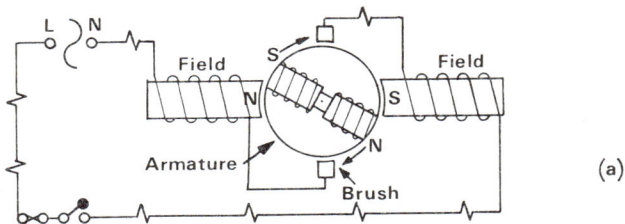

(a)

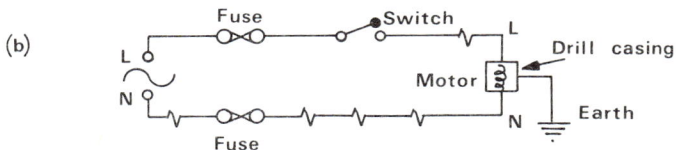

(b)

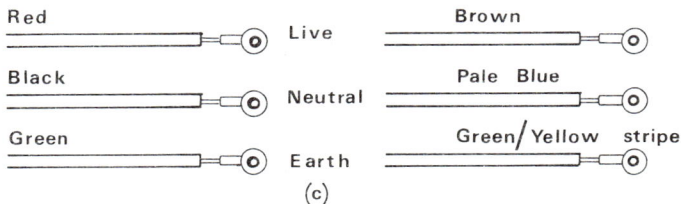

(c)

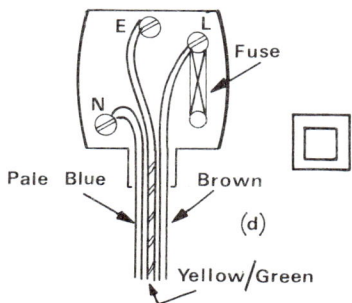

(d)

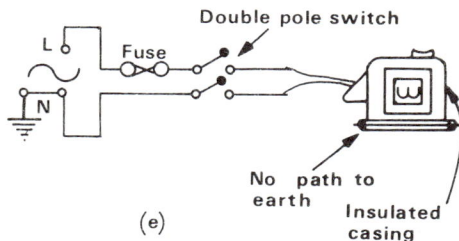

(e)

e Double Insulated tools require no
earth wire for the neutral return is
earthed at power station. There is no
electrical path between motor and
casing.

will be up to 35 mm, but again this will depend on the power available, the
saw condition and the material being cut.

The attachment for sawing will have a flat sole plate capable of being
tilted to 45°, and a fence unit for parallel cutting. All angles and cutting
widths within the capacity are marked for easy setting. The sole plate will
adjust up or down to limit depth of cut, which should always, for safety and
efficiency, be as little as possible. A saw cuts better on its extreme rim.

The saws available have teeth shaped to cut either along or across the
grain, or for combination cutting. Fine tooth saws for soft material are
available and saws with long lasting tungsten carbide tips are made, but are
expensive. Many saws are coated with polytetrafluoroethylene (P.T.F.E.),
which is black in colour. The proprietary names of TEFLON and XYLAN are
applied to this material, which has an exceptionally low friction value. Its
purpose is to prevent stickiness on the saw blade and to prevent rust.

Saw units may be used for: ripsawing, cross-cutting, bevel and chamfer
sawing, rabbeting, grooving, tongueing, or housing. The fence unit in conjunction with the depth stop, control width and depth of cut. The pivoting
sole allows bevel cutting. At the leading end of the sole there are two
notches. One is the line indicator for position when the sole is used flat. The
other gives a guiding sight point when the sole is tilted. At all times the saw
should project the minimum distance possible below the sole.

Fig. 46 illustrates the drill unit used with the sawing attachments and indicates the general idea of setting for special jobs.

THE SANDING UNIT
This uses the power pack to provide power for an ORBITAL sander. The
drill frame locks into an approximately rectangular attachment that has a
flat-cushioned base on to which is clamped a sheet of abrasive paper.

The rotation of the motor gives an orbital (circular) motion to the sanding pad. The rotation diameter is approximately 4 mm. By progressive
use of paper diminishing in grit size, a job is easily produced having a flat
paintable or polishable surface. Papers used for the initial cutting down
should be those known as OPEN COAT, a range of papers having the
abrasive particles widely spread. For final smoothing CLOSE COAT abrasive
sheets are used and these have the abrasive tightly packed. Wet sanding or
cutting down is not the job for electric sanders—use only dry
papers—water and electricity do not mix.

Heavy pressure is not required—the abrasive should be allowed to do its
own work. Move the tool as a hand-papering block would be used—in
short up and down strokes. Lift away from the job to start and stop. This
avoids scratching.

Fig. 46.

a The saw unit may be used for rip-sawing and for rabbeting with the guide set to control cutting widths.

b Tapered legs are marked and then cut, working to waste sides of lines.

c Large sheets may be cut if batten guides are cramped on.

d To cut housings a guide batten is cramped on and a spacing piece used for the second cut. The waste is then chiselled out.

e A wooden 'square-guide' is useful for cutting to length. The guide may be made angled for a quantity of angled cuts.

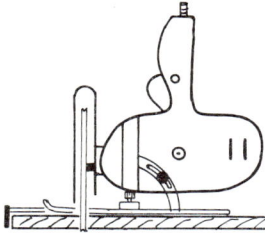

(a)

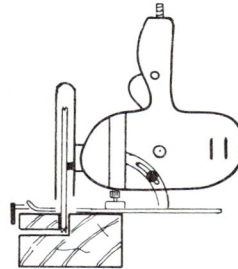

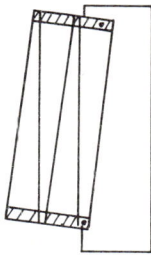

(b)

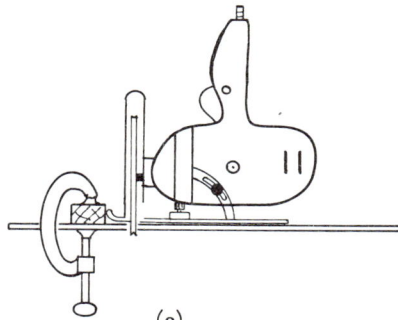

(c)

(e)

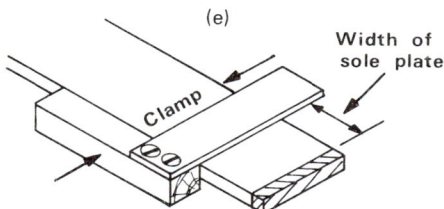

Width of sole plate

Clamp

(d)

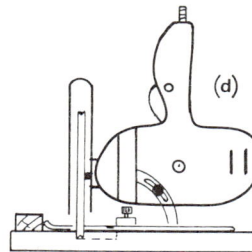

Loose piece

THE JIGSAW

This attachment converts the rotation of the power-pack motor into a reciprocating one. The attachment has a sole plate with a forked front end. Between the arms of the forks, the saw reciprocates up and down with its toothed edge leading. Saws may be fine or coarse, the fine teeth being used for thin sheet material and the coarse ones being used for solid wood.

The purpose of the attachment is to cut shapes. A pencil line is drawn and the tool is moved to follow it. Cuts must be towards one side of the line, the waste side, and the saw must not be forced around curves that are too small in radius. Rest the extended forked sole on the material before switching on, and switch off and wait for the saw to stop moving before lifting away from the job. Internal shapes are best started by pre-boring a hole for saw entry. By tilting the unit it is possible to start an internal cut without an entrance hole but there is the risk of bending the saw.

OTHER ATTACHMENTS

Many other attachments are available but the purchase of each will depend on the amount it is expected to be used; the saw, sander and jigsaw are general purpose and use is easily found for them.

The drill may, as a drill, be fitted to a vertical drill PRESS (stand) where it may then be used by hand lever as a drilling machine. Screw-driving attachments may be fitted in place of the drill chuck but they are hardly warranted unless large numbers of screws must be run in.

The drill may be clamped horizontal and grinding wheels, sanding discs and polishing mops held, on small arbors, in the chuck. Dovetailing attachments make box-making easy, but they are an expensive one purpose tool.

Lathe stands, circular saw stands, and mortising stands convert the drill unit into a miniature woodworking machine.

All of the above extra attachments have a part to play but the first purchase should always be a good drill unit followed by the saw, the sander and the jigsaw. The horizontal clamp with a grinding wheel arbor would probably come next, but so much depends on the range of work to be attempted.

SPECIAL PURPOSE POWER TOOLS

These perform the same function as the drill power pack and attachments, but are more convenient in use as they require no change-over time. They are more comfortable to hold, and in most cases, have more power.

The specials available are: saw units up to 150 mm (6 in.) dia.; jigsaw units with pivoting sole plates; orbital, belt, and disc sanders; grinders, routers and screw drivers.

LOW VOLT WORKING

For safe working on building sites voltage for portable tools is dropped by transformer to 110 volts. If the home woodworker decides to use all special purpose tools, these are all available at 110 volts, but it means that a special transformer must be purchased.

*Without wood, growing as trees, and no longer growing, as timber,
our environment would be different. And an environment without
timber is one that carries frightening implications; we are, now, at
this moment, working our way steadily towards such an environment—a world without wood.*

*So versatile is it as a material that it is almost man's first thought
when he has to solve the problem of making something. But man's imagination and skills are applied at such a fast rate that the world's
wood cannot grow fast enough to keep up. The answer lies in substitu-
tion, imitation, adaptation and conservation.*

*Trees are planted, jobs are studied and re-designed to minimise
wood content, substitutes are developed, man-made boards are made,
but all the time the demand for wood grows.*

*Now what can we do to help. We can use timber carefully, we can
'feel' for it, we can learn to love it.*

The above is rather a strange preface to a chapter on 'Wood', but after
working with wood for forty years perhaps a man may be forgiven for in-
dulging his first love, and for trying to instil this love for a material into any
one who handles it, be they full-time craftsman, apprentice, or the home
woodworker.

WOOD—THE MATERIAL

In Chapter One, WOOD (or TIMBER) was introduced. Its method of growth
was explained, and its methods of conversion and use was outlined. But
wood, as a natural material, varies from tree to tree, from area to area, from
species to species. This is the beauty of it.

Some will be kind and friendly, some will be tough and unbending and
resist all efforts. Some again will be brutally brittle and harsh to the man
that tries to charm them into use. The good worker will learn to know and
understand the very nature of timber, he will learn to frustrate the tricks of
grain and colour. He will learn to make and shape, to join and to finish, and
in the end his skill, his efforts, his creative ability, will have bent the wood
into something that will, above all else, go once more to prove that there is
NO SUBSTITUTE FOR WOOD.

DESCRIPTIONS

REDWOOD, called **Yellow Deal.** A softwood,* yellow to cream in colour,

* 'Softwood' is timber that grows from trees that have 'needle' leaves: Pines, Firs,
Spruces, Christmas Trees etc. It is, in general, softer and lighter than 'Hardwood', the
timber that grows from 'Broad' leaf trees. This is the coloured wood, the hard and dense and
sometimes intractable wood.

with whitish sapwood. Brown to golden in knots, silky smooth in finish, with a 'swistle' from the sharp plane that cuts it; the 'swistle' that matches the hiss of the ski as it glides along on the compact snow that lies on the slopes where the softwoods grow. Stable in nature, easy to saw, plane, shape, nail and screw. Superb for painting and glueing. Very usable alike for construction or for joinery. Suitable for 'white' furniture that glows under a clear silky lacquer. Reasonably plentiful in supply and is in fact the 'Jack of all Trades' as a material. Use it carefully and well.

DOUGLAS FIR, called Oregon Pine, or Columbian Pine. A softwood, rather more coarse than redwood, but tougher and more ridged in grain. With a salmon pink colour, it carries a pungent resin smell. More difficult to smooth to a fine finish, but durable, stable and attractive. Screws with care, nails with disaster in slim sections, for it easily splits. Sharp splinters for unwary fingers. It will receive paint in an acceptable manner, and clear gloss lacquer with gratitude to exhibit its attractions. Knots are few but large and occasionally large and black—in fact, dead. Douglas Fir is not easily found today.

SPRUCE, named white deal. A woolly softwood, spongy in places. Dead white in colour, and 'dead' means lifeless with no sparkle, not the 'dead white' of brilliant white. Large in size for wide boards, carrying plentiful 'NAIL' knots slender in diameter but penetrating through the board. Such knots are either 'dead' or 'alive'. When 'dead' they are black and loose, when 'live' they are golden brown and fastly held. Numerous resin ducts make it sticky in places. Works easily apart from smooth finishing. Strong in section, stable in shape. Very useful for wood trim, stairs, steps and general repairs. It takes paint and needs it although it scrubs white for plain tables.

HEMLOCK, another softwood, sometimes called just FIR. Coarse, woolly, brittle and spiteful. Beware of splinters and splits. Dull pink to brown with black knots. Unstable and unrewarding in appearance. For structures it is in its element, a strong standing tree producing strong standing timber. Found in lofts and between floors. Some very clear boards are found and these go into door production.

PARANA PINE, a fine softwood but feminine in that it varies in shape, texture and touch. Yellow to brown in colour, it livens its apperance with a touch of bright red; long swirling streaks of it fading and re-appearing

---

But like timber, as it always is, the very classifications defy the woodworker. Some hardwoods are softer than some softwoods and some softwoods are harder than hardwoods. So forget such classifications. Choose the wood with the nature to comply with your intention.

along the wide clear boards. When yellow it glows with pride from a sharp tool, when brown it is dull and dismal. Very brittle in length and subject to fine hair-like cracks across the grain. These are called *thunder shakes* and must not be trusted. It will, again like a woman, respond well to all the attention it receives—cutting, smoothing, glueing, painting, polishing, nailing and screwing, but—it will turn at the slightest whim. Trust it not. Cut it, shape it, and get it into the job before it turns and twists. It is the most unstable of all the softwoods and will show its disapproval of outdoor life by rotting quickly away.

THE HARDWOODS
Hardwoods make hard cases. They are mostly tough and resistant and require care and skill in use, but for all that they are rewarding. They shine, they smell, they give colour and they (mostly) give durability. Some twist and turn and will not lie. Discretion in their use is essential.

OAK, made famous by the ships that sailed the sea and cleared the land of forests. Oak is like a popular chancellor's budget, it has something for everyone. To fence your land—ideal; to prevent access with decorum but with certainty—majestic. It will lend itself to gentle designs or robust designs. It will age with beauty or age with the strident proclamation of its strength and endurance. It can be found everywhere—in joinery, in furniture, in old cathedrals and in modern flats—but not alas, standing in a forest. Oak has been used so much that very little is obtainable, and then most likely, it will be Japanese, a less spectacular wood.

Oak is red, oak is brown, oak is white. It comes mainly brown but varies. Coarse or fine, straight grained or curly, plain or figured. You name it, oak has it, character, texture and solidity. Select it well and it will do exactly as you wish. Saw, cut, plane, shape, glue, stain, nail and screw.* Polish to high gloss, matt to an inner glow, but do not paint. Choose oak and you choose well.

BEECH. A cousin of oak you might say; a real forest wood. Strong, willing and co-operative. It is creamy to white in nature, but turns pink with the steam used to mellow it and make it less brittle and hard. If beech is pink it has been steamed, if it is white, it is natural. Both woods are usable, but the pink one is best for home use. Beech has very few knots or indeed faults at all. Its weakness is in its appearance. No lively grain here, no spectacular swirls and curls, just plain unbroken surfaces. It is a furniture wood, for it cuts, stains, joins and polishes well. It will do most

---

* The strength of steel and the strength of oak alas conflict. The iron of the steel rots the oak; the acid of the oak corrodes the steel. Do not marry these two stalwarts—use instead brass or galvanised steel screws.

things for the woodworker, for it is in good supply and is economic in that very little is waste. It will *not* agree to exposure. Dampness breaks its heart; it rots away. It greys with wind and rain and its face gives way to hair line cracks. Paint will not protect it, for the years condemn.

RAMIN, a tropical wood, yellow to cream, brittle to use. A valuable wood, clean grain, straight and wide. No knots, no defects but the one—it splits. Cut and plane with sharp tools; glue and stain with care. Screw, nail, paper and polish and the job is done. It will not move after construction, but will require aids to beauty; it must be stained, like beech, to the shades of oak, mahogany and walnut. A splendid timber to run through the mill.

MAHOGANY. A doubtful one this; it has so many close cousins and so many imitators that its true self is not often found in stores. Good mahogany is a perfect friend to both the joiner and furniture man. With a soft red/brown colour and wild swirling grain, goes strength, durability and a willingness to participate in a joint project with man. No more need be said. If a red/brown timber is required and mahogany is available, use it and enjoy the job and live with the product.

But the others—UTILE, SAPELE, RED MERANTI. These are the ones to use with discretion. Beautiful and rich in colour and grain, their very nature makes them lurk to trap the unwary. Utile and Sapele have a wine red presence. They glow when polished. But there's the rub. To bring to a surface acceptable to polish requires great care in planing, then scraping, then sanding. Their grain is often INTERLOCKED, which means that their grain is indeed interlocked, no more than a few rows of growth being in the same direction. Growth twirls to the left and twists again to the right creating light and dark streaks that show when the board is cut along the tree centre. If planed from one end alternate rows of grain will be with and against the cut. If plain sawn neither wood wants to stay flat. However, by selecting straight grain boards and addressing them with sharp tools they are workable and rewarding in end product. They will happily receive all the things that you will need to do to them.

RED MERANTI. Dark brown to red. Dull as member of the red-type woods, but beguiling with the ease with which it works. It is a very gummy wood. Used as a substitute for mahogany it will satisfy but not elate. It has a cousin (it has in fact two hundred or more, for it belongs to the large family *Shorea*) a cousin in texture but yellow in colour. This is called WHITE MERANTI. Useful but inclined to harbour many black pin holes; unsightly, but not to be feared. Worms will not appear. Use this for hidden rails in carcase work.

GOLDEN WALNUT. As golden as its name implies but as gay a deceiver as the iron pyrites that fools call gold. It has no relationship to walnut at all, other than in being wood. Take an African-type mahogany and stain it golden brown and you have golden walnut. Its grain, texture (feel) and general behaviour are the same as those of utile and sapele. It has one featural difference; black streaks are sometimes shown. Like woman again (as so many woods are) it looks glorious when time has been spent in preparing the surface for presentation.

TEAK. Think of toughness, think of durability; teak has them both. Yet most easy to work. Fresh cut it is green but quickly turns to an almost chocolate brown with a golden undertone. Teak has few knots and few splits. For the joiner it has a long, long life in almost any surround. For the cabinet maker it offers a material whose attractiveness will overcome most poor designs yet surpasses itself if design 'clicks' with its nature.

Teak has its faults. It is most pricey; it is in short supply, it is abrasive to tool edges, and needs careful glueing with synthetic resin. It is not strong in small section, and it will not please those who enjoy reflection from furniture. To finish teak, matt finishes are best. Either seal with a varnish seal and then rub with wax and wire wool, or use teak-oil, a drying varnish that takes several days to dry and needs several applications. Rub down between coats with oily abrasive paper. Probably the best finish is obtained by coating with matt or egg-shell polyurethane varnish, finishing with wax. Never, ever, paint.

AGBA. Pink—yellow, plain and gummy. Easy to work. No grain worth consideration, but a useful wood for all that. It will do all that you need and will if stained carefully, make an oak, walnut or mahogany job.

OBECHE. Soft and yellow. No life, no nature. Dusty, dull and dismal—but—it grows wide, it grows long, it stays flat and it is easy to use. It is very light in weight and ideal for carcase work where no great strength is required. Tenons must be fairly thick. It will stain and polish but not well for its absorption is uneven. Yet for all its faults one of the tree family and useful in its place.

THE GREATER FAMILY

The few timbers surveyed are but few of those available to man. They are, however, those that are reasonably available to the home woodworker. The commercial exploiter has an almost unlimited family of uncles, aunts, cousins, nephews, nieces and oddly mixed up peculiars to call on. The study of wood is a life's work alone.

But, out of interest, just read through this list of poetic, tongue twisting and down-right peculiar names, and you will find there enough food for thought. There is no end to the story of wood:

Port Orford Cedar, *Ulmus alata,* Bubinga, Seraya, and Ash. Sequoia, Ebony, Holly, Chestnut and *Thuya plicata.* Podocarpus, Willow, Elm, Tiama, Walnut and Boja. Blackheart, Padauk, Rosewood, Pinkodo, Jarrah and Lime. Laurel, Lauan, Wenge, Camwood and Cocus. Caryota, Black Bean, Sycamore, Pitchpine, Whitebean and Yang. Persimmon, Flowering Dogwood, Sandlewood, Kauri, Lancewood and Lignum. Loblolly Pine, Stinkwood, Zebrano and Prima Vera.

THE PRINCIPLES

Woodworking by machine is the easiest way to do the job. However, the machines are expensive and require knowledge and skill in use.

Industrial machines are too heavy for home use, but there are machines specially designed for the home worker who has money and space to devote to his hobby. The principles on which the light machines are based are identical to those on which the larger machines are based, and these principles are largely derived from the original hand processes.

SAWING

Sawing is done with circular saws or bandsaws. The circular saw is a flat steel disc, with a centre hole and teeth forward around the circumference. The bandsaw is an endless steel strip, toothed on one edge. It is fitted to the wheels of the machine and work is offered to the down cutting teeth and is supported by a flat work table.

CIRCULAR SAWING

Machines for circular sawing must have a minimum of equipment: the saw table, on which work is fed, the guide fence along which the work is fed, the TOP GUARD, a crown cover which covers the unused top part of the saw circle; and the RIVING KNIFE, a curved steel knife which acts as a guard behind the saw, where the teeth are coming upwards out of the bench.

The saw itself will have teeth shaped to rip, cross-cut, or mitre saw, and if finance runs to it, these teeth will be tipped with tungsten carbide. A fine tooth, with carbide tip, will cut timber sheet material such as plywood, and also give a very fine finish to the edge of cut laminated plastic. Carbide-tipped teeth are not suitable for metal cutting.

The Teeth

As with handsaws, cross-cutting teeth will have a negative hook and have their teeth extremities shaped to needle points.

Ripsaws will lean forward and have chisel points. Saws for general work will have neutral angles (in between cross-cut and rip) and sheet material saws will have a large number of small teeth rather than a small number of large teeth.

The saw plate must be flat and teeth must have side clearance. If a saw gets out of condition it may easily be put back again into top condition if it is taken to a saw doctor for treatment.

Bevel sawing, rabbetting, grooving and rip and cross-cut sawing all come within the scope of the saw-bench.

Fig. 47 shows the outline of the saw-bench and gives examples of saw work and saw teeth.

Fig. 47.

a At the top half of the page are shown variations in use of the small sawbench illustrated. These are: ripsawing, cross-cutting; bevel and chamfer sawing, and rabbeting.

b The lower half of the page shows use of saw for wedge cutting, tapered leg cutting, and tenon cutting.

c Illustrates three common forms of saw teeth.

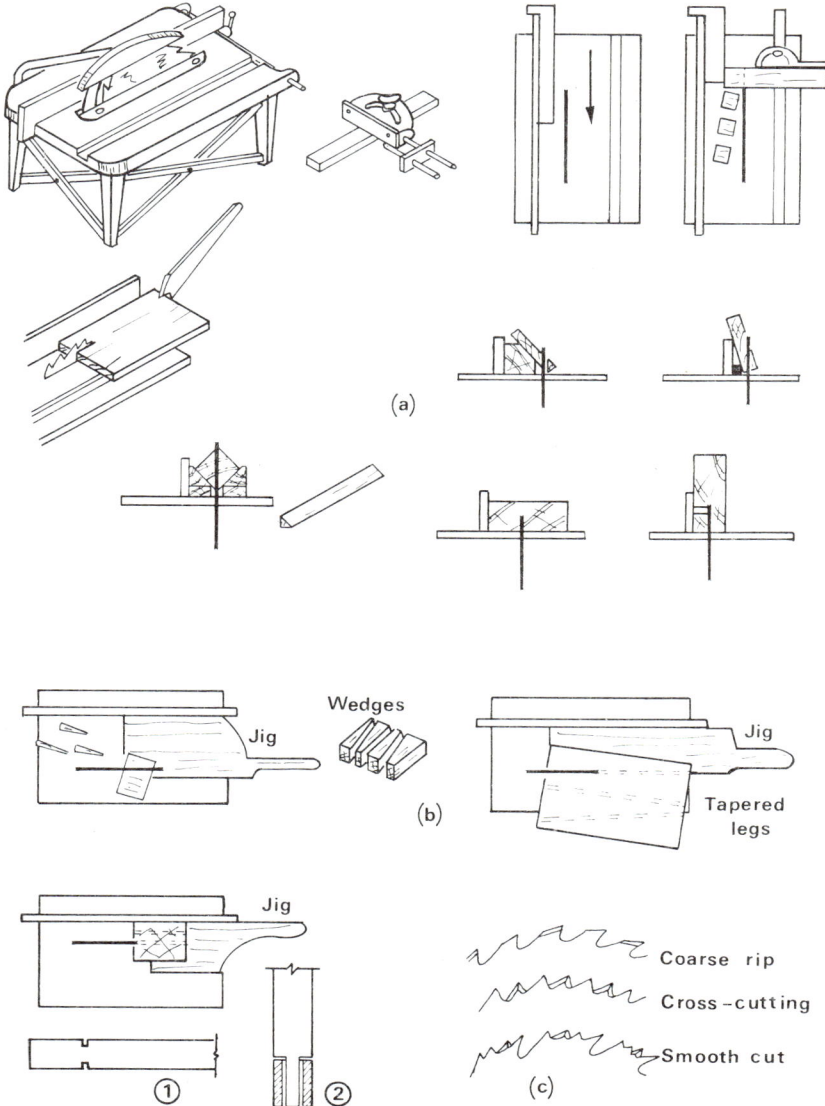

(a)

(b)

Wedges

Jig

Tapered legs

Jig

①　②

Coarse rip

Cross–cutting

Smooth cut

(c)

THE BANDSAW

Large bandsaws may be up to 6 metres long but the home-use machine seldom uses saws longer than 1.25 metres and these are very thin and no more than 8 mm wide. Their teeth are a compromise. The metal is dead hard, so that the teeth cannot be filed, and the teeth are so fine that they will cut plastic laminate without leaving edge chips. Such a saw will cut plastic, wood, hardboard, sheet brass, sheet aluminium and thin mild steel. Having such fine teeth, cutting is slow, for the gullets clog. But as they will handle most home materials, speed in cutting is reasonably sacrificed.

To gain a clear THROAT, which is the distance between the saw and the machine frame, these small machines have a three wheel system where the saw runs round a 150 mm diameter rubber tyred top wheel, then straight down to a 100 mm nylon wheel, which is the driver. From here the saw goes across to another 150 mm wheel and then back to the top wheel. Guides track the saw. The work table may be tilted for bevel cuts. It is possible to remove all saw guides and to run a narrow band of coated abrasive around the wheels for the purpose of sanding the edges of shapes and into corners.

PLANING

Bench planers are used for flatting, edging, bevelling, rebating and tapering, but they are not usually able to bring material to a required thickness.

Their principle is that if a piece of material is placed on a flat table it will come to rest on its high points. It is these high points that must be removed to make the board flat. Thus if the board is moved with no disturbance it will travel along the straight line of the table on which it rests. If a cutting block is set in the table with its edge above the level of the table, the high spots will be cut off as the work passes. To support the newly flat surface a second table is positioned behind the cutting block. As the work progresses it will have been riding its high points. These have been successfully removed by the cutters, so the rear table, positioned after the block, is set level with this line of cut. Now the material will move from one table to the other, starting with an out-of-flat surface and finishing with a flat planed surface.

At the back of the flattening tables there is an upright fence, against which the workpiece is placed and held for the purpose of square planing one edge.

This fence may be tilted to produce bevelled edges. If it (the fence) is moved towards the front edge of the table and the front table be lowered, rabbets may be cut on the outer end of the cutting block.

The Block

The cutting blocks of planers are circular and carry two, or three, cutters. The block rotates at high speed. The size of the machine is denoted by the length of the cutting block, which for bench mounted planers may vary from 100 to 250 mm.

The gap between the tables is covered by a bridging guard and it is advisable that all material being surfaced should pass below this.

To bring material to thickness on such a planer it is necessary to surface and edge, then to pass the material, width and thickness, through a circular saw. Then a fine cut, adjustable by rising the in-feeding table of the planer, is made on both sawn edges. The workpiece will now be flat and parallel in width and thickness, and have both edges square to both faces.

THE MORTISER

Machine-made mortises are cut by large machines that use various methods for cutting square-ended holes. The drill unit, provided that it is large enough, say a 12 mm drill, may be fitted into a drill press stand with extra attachments for mortising. The tool is fitted to the drill and the workpiece is held into position below the down-pointing tool end.

By means of the drill press hand lever, the chisel is brought down to the workpiece, where it cuts a square hole. Repeating this as the workpiece is moved along produces a rectangular mortise.

The mortising tool is called the HOLLOW CHISEL and AUGER BIT. The chisel is square in section with a centre hole bored through it from end to end. There are windows in its sides to allow chips to escape. This chisel is clamped firmly to the drill casing. Through the centre of the chisel runs the auger bit. This looks like a jennings bit but it has no centre screw or bradpoint. The centre screw of the jennings serves two purposes: (1) to pull the bit into the work, and (2) to provide a centre on which the bit is to rotate as it penetrates.

The mortise auger runs in the chisel so that it does not require the centre point for location—the chisel sides support it. If there was a screw-threaded centre point, the rotation of the drill would cause such rapid in-feed that the bit would choke.

The auger cuts a circular hole and the chisel, following closely, cuts away four corners to produce a square. The bulk of the work is done by the auger.

Chisels sets may be bought from 6 mm square up to 38 mm square but the 12 mm drill unit is best limited to chisels of 18 mm.

A further use for the drill press is to use it as a pedestal drill. For mortising, a series of holes could be bored and then the remaining core be removed by chiselling.

THE MYFORD WOODWORKER

This is a sturdy home-use, or light industrial-use woodworking machine. The machine is based on a woodworking lathe—the 'Myford ML8', and by means of additional attachments, it is made to do a very wide range of cutting jobs. Its scope is limited only to the scope of the attachments available, and to the ingenuity of the user in exploiting such attachments.

Woodturning lathes need little explanation; the workpiece is spun rapidly between centres and the turner cuts it to shape, resting his gouges and chisels on a tool rest that is set alongside the rotating wood. One end of the lathe, the headstock, drives the work and has the motor unit close to it. The tail end of the work is held by the tailstock, which consists of a sliding head that adjusts to the work length and holds it freely on a conical back centre.

The 'Myford' lathe is designed to take: polishing adaptors to carry polishing mops for metal or plastic; a grinding arbor on which to run a grinding wheel; a long-boring fitment to enable table-lamp stems to be bored through; a disc sanding unit with mitre fence, a circular sawing table, fence, saw and guard; a mortising complex that has a built-in workpiece clamp; a table slide and an in-feed control lever—this particular piece of equipment may be used for horizontal boring and square chisel mortising, slot mortising, or routing (milling as it is called in America), and, if the right cutters are available, small mouldings; a planing attachment that will face and edge wood and then plane it to width and thickness, and if required, cut rabbets, bevels, chamfers and tenons; and finally, a bandsaw unit having 250 mm diameter wheels and a cutting depth of 93 mm.

Each of these pieces of equipment operate as machines in their own right (except for the long borer, which operates as part of the lathe set-up) and some of them may be combined in use so that wood may be sawn, and then planed without altering anything.

The real problem with such a unit as the ML8 is the cost of all the attachments, plus the storage of them. Pre-planing of the job enables systematic change-overs but some time is inevitably lost in changing from planer to bandsaw and so on.

The ideal exploitation of the ML8 would be achieved by the hobby woodworker (and light metal worker) if space was available for a planned layout of attachments, room to work, and an interest in the mechanical making of things from wood—the real hobbyist in fact. Coupled with a few power tools (drill and sander units) together with a spraying outfit a real home workshop would be achieved.

DOVETAILING

Dovetailing is really part of the drill power-pack system, but because the controlling guides and clamping system is not actually fitted to the drill but works as a separate unit, it is best thought of as a machine alone.

The 'Stanley-Bridges' AR/DV dovetailing unit will cut dovetails in box or drawer sides and ends, from 10 mm to 25 mm thick with a PITCH (the distance from centre to centre of adjacent tails) of 18 mm. Three size cutters are available and this enables correct matching of dovetail shape to the material thickness.

The system operates with almost any 6 mm drill. A horizontal plate lays parallel to the bench top and has its own bridge clamp to lock down the box side that is to be cut with pins (tails). The other part of the joint, the piece into which the sockets are to be cut, is held in a vertical clamp against the bench face.

The unit is held to the bench with hand-screw clamps. In front of the unit there is a vertical COMB, the teeth of which form the divisions between the dovetails.

The drill unit is fitted with a chuck adaptor that carries the dovetail cutter, a rolling guide to run into the comb, and a guide handle for control.

There is no setting-up required other than that of positioning the unit. The piece to be tailed—say a drawer side, is pushed in from the bench top against the comb and is then clamped. The drawer-front is pushed up from the bench side until it butts against the previously positioned side. Then the drill unit has the cutter and guide fitted and the job is almost done. The drill is successively fed into the slots of the comb. The depth of the socket is controlled by the relationship between the bench plate and the comb plate, which is varied by simple slide adjustment.

So much has been said in various places, by various people, about the 'right ways' and 'wrong ways' of construction, that it has become difficult to reconcile much of the conflicting advice or to adapt it to the job in hand.

There is NO right way or wrong way to do a job if it is planned to take advantage of the strength of the materials and to avoid reliance on its weakness. Tenons, generally, should not be more than one third of the section thickness, nor have their shoulders undercut. Mating surfaces should mate and thus minimise glue-line thickness. End-grain exposure should be kept out of sight and out of damp. Wide solid boards should be arranged to allow for movement (shrinkage) and the edges of chipboard be protected.

The sketch outlines which follow start with an idea for a cabinet construction kit. Various grooved sections are keyed together and then panelled with hardboard; or a grooved section may be screwed to a wall and construction then built outwards. With this system there is complete freedom to erect a cupboard front and then fit-out its interior in any way required. The only defect of the system is that the interior appearance is unsightly, but it is quick, cheap, and rigid. See Fig. 48.

The other ideas shown are simply indications of jobs that the average home woodworker should be able to tackle. Some drawings have full instructions and dimensions and others show only outlines. The reason for this is to allow variation of design. Once the technique of planning from sketches is grasped then routines will be identical for most jobs. Some dimensions must be standard to fit human beings; tables should be from 700 mm to 780 mm high; chair seats from 430 mm to 460 mm, and so on.

GENERAL PROCESS

Sketch	Sand internal faces
Draw—Set-out	Prepare cramps
Make cutting list	Glue and Assemble
Prepare material to size	Cramp—Square-up
Mark Out	Wedge—Pin—Screw
Mortise—Tenon—Dovetail—House	Wipe off surplus glue
Plough—Groove—Mould	Final sand when cured
Fit Dry	Fit sub-assemblies together
Adjust joints	Polish—Paint

THE SUGGESTIONS

Fig 48. Grooved Construction Sections

The only tool essential here is the electric saw. If this is not available try to buy as many variations of grooved section as is possible. Whatever happens, the keys must be a knock-in glued fit. Bend the electric saw teeth

Fig. 48.

The sections shown here are approximately 30 mm × 18 mm and should have a standard 3.5 mm groove 6 mm deep and 4 mm from the face edge. The triangular keys are 3.5 mm hardboard and must be a 'knock-in' fit. It may be necessary sometimes to cut key away around legs at corners, or to cut all exposed part of key away at an opening.

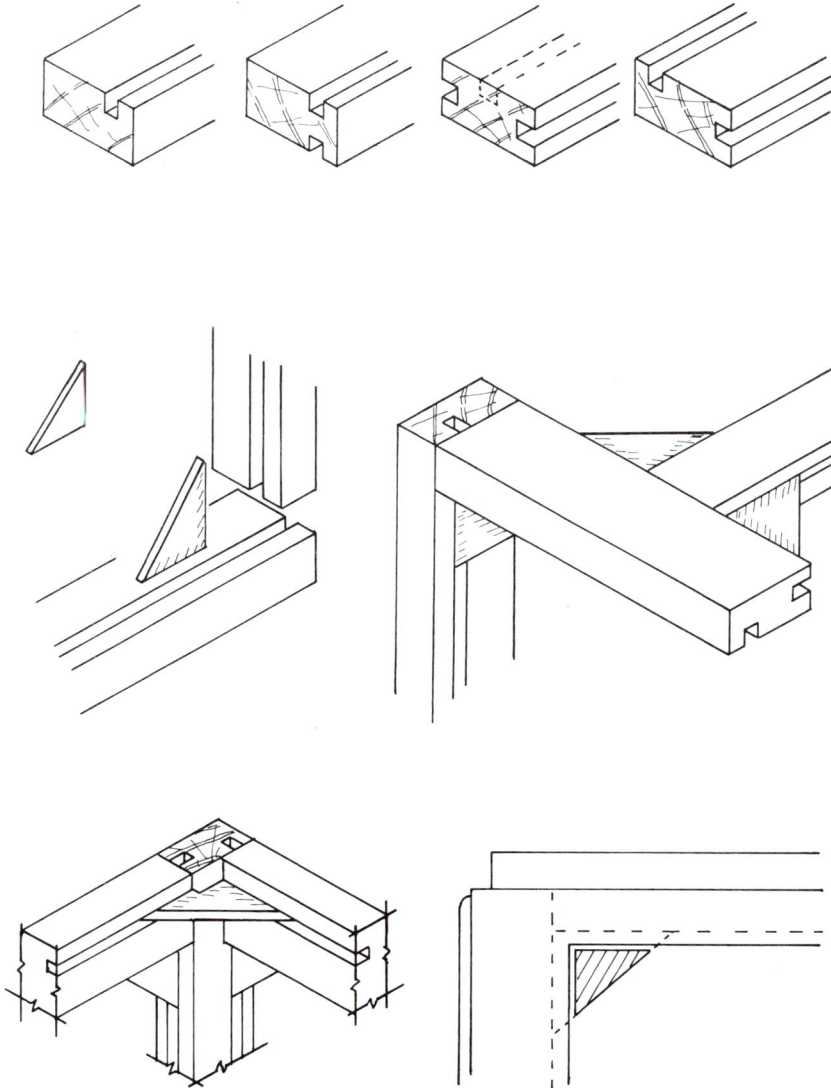

Fig. 49.
a This represents a simple and elegant table.
b 1 to 6 show construction details and dimensions.
c Draw construction may be dovetailed, lapped, dowelled, or may be with 'knock-down' fittings.

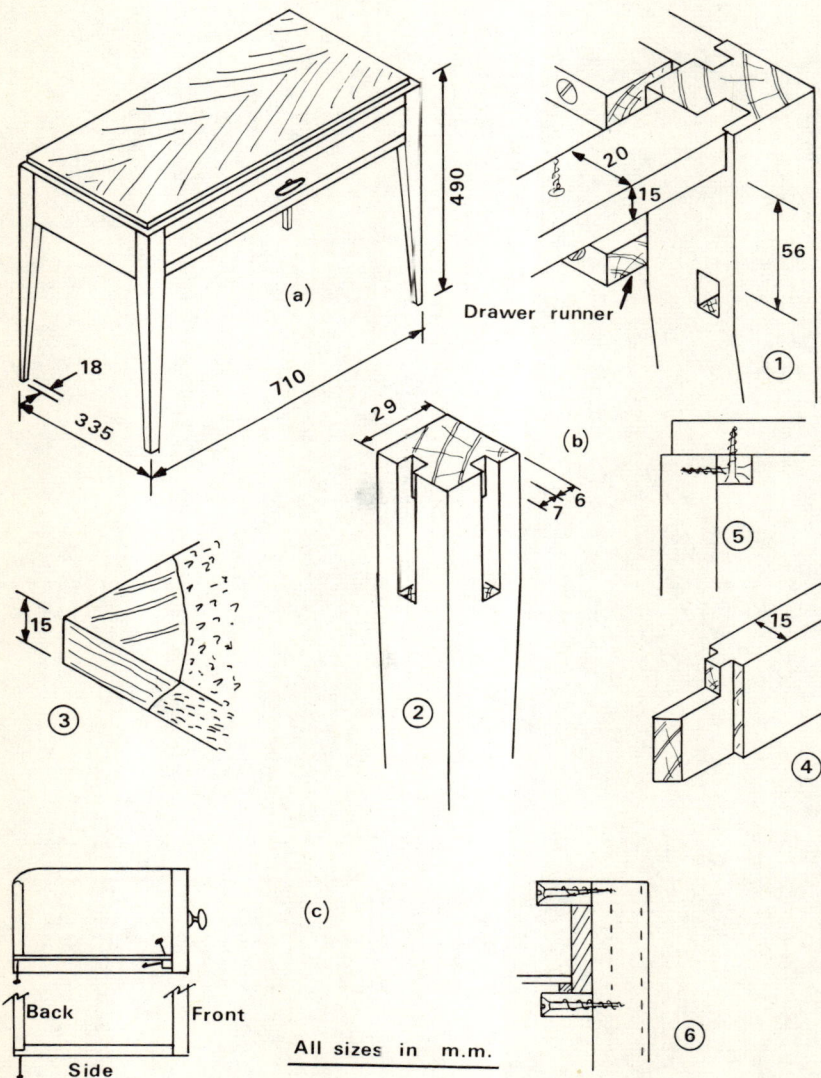

(a)

490

18

710

335

(b)

20

15

56

Drawer runner

①

29

6

7

②

15

15

③

⑤

④

Back   Front

Side

(c)

All sizes in m.m.

⑥

152

Fig. 50.
This bookshelf may be solid wood or
veneered chipboard. Dimensions should
suit requirements. The back may be
veneered plywood or Vinyl faced hardboard (woodgrain).

Paper – back size 175mm X 110mm

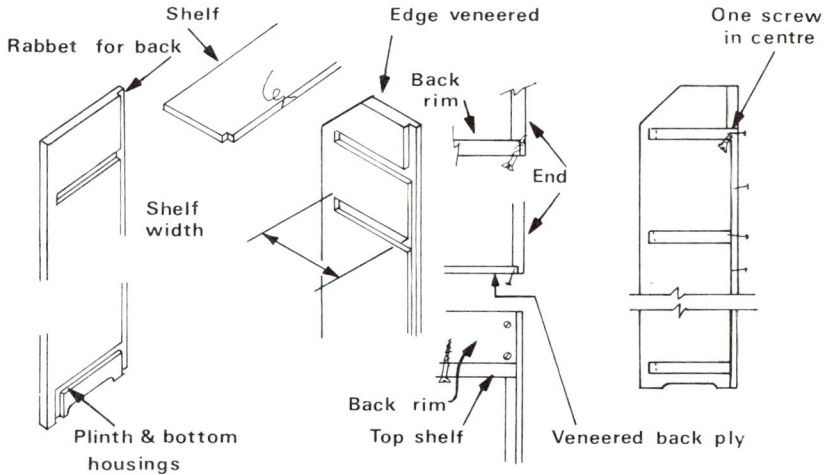

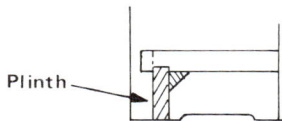

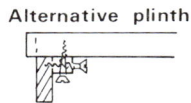

Shelf

Rabbet for back

Edge veneered

One screw
in centre

Back
rim

Shelf
width

End

Plinth & bottom
housings

Back rim

Top shelf

Veneered back ply

Plinth

Alternative plinth

18mm Material

153

Fig. 51.
Simple household steps in Parana Pine,
all at 18 mm thick. Treads may be glued
and screwed, or glued and nailed with
cut nails.

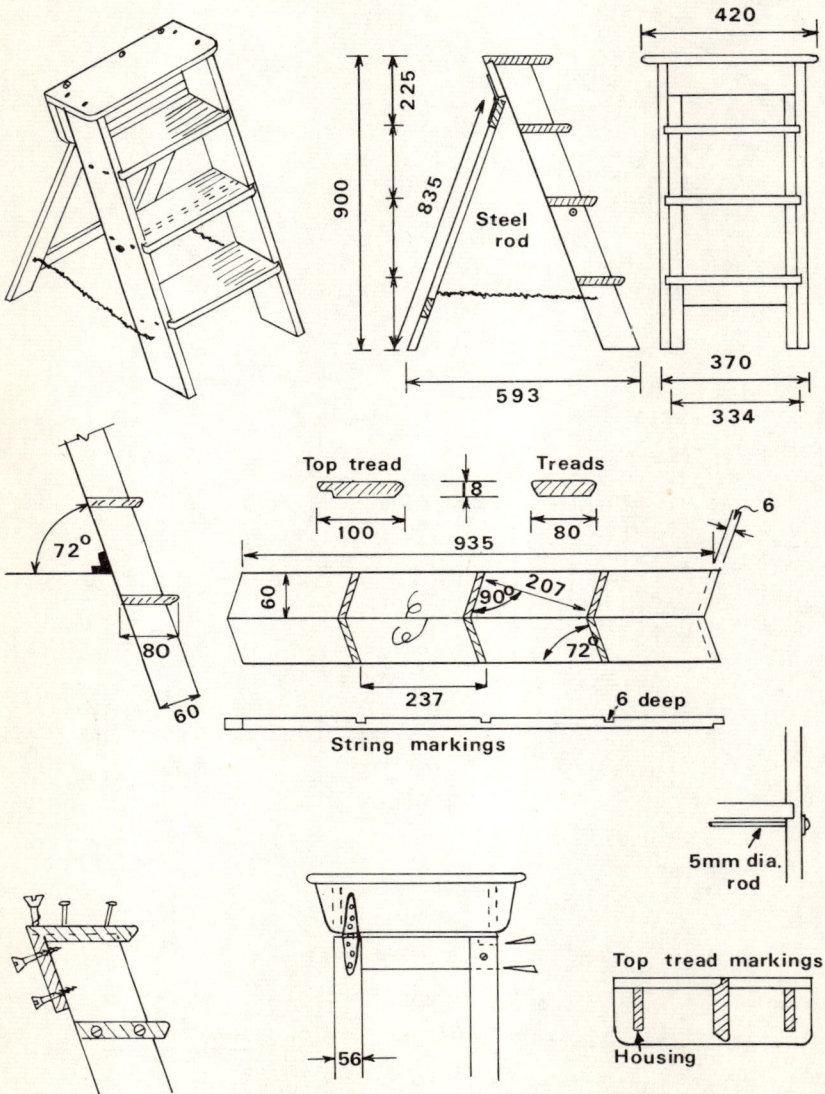

225

900

835

Steel
rod

593

420

370

334

72°

80

60

Top tread

100

8

Treads

80

935

6

60

90° 207

237

72°

6 deep

String markings

5mm dia.
rod

56

Top tread markings

Housing

Fig. 52.
This simple window frame may be made
from standard sections. To avoid error
both a height and width rod should be
made. Glue with synthetic glue.

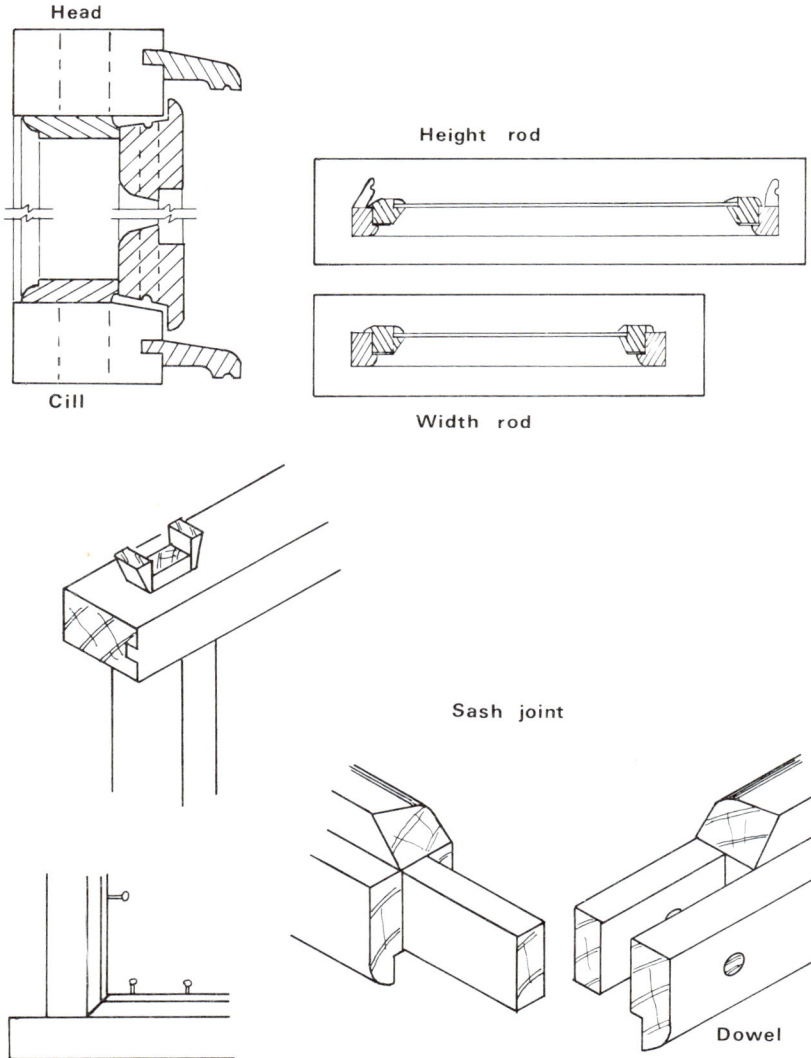

Head

Cill

Height rod

Width rod

Sash joint

Dowel

outwards until cut is correct at 3·5 mm. Re-set for correct cutting clearance when grooves have been made.

Fig. 49. Light Table
Traditional joints here, apart from the drawer which may be constructed to suit tools and skills available.

Fig. 50. Book Shelves
A basic woodworking project either in solid wood or veneered chipboard. If chipboard, top ends of the two ends must be veneered with iron-on narrow veneer strip. The back may be omitted but housings must be a very good fit to secure strength. Material sizes will depend on book sizes.

Fig. 51. Household Steps
This simple step-ladder may be extended in size by one extra step. If a higher pair of steps is required then width should be increased to 400 and string thickness increased to 20 or 22. Treads may be nailed with cut nails rather than screwed. The tie rod should be brought down to the lowest step if overall height is increased.

Fig. 52. Window Frame Construction
There are more complex ways of constructing windows but the manner shown is sound and waterproof. All joints must be glued with synthetic resin or well painted during assembly. Sash may be hung with rabbeted sash hinges or with extended 'EASY·CLEAN' pivots.

Fig. 53. Cupboard Fronts for Recesses
This suggestion shows a reasonably easy method of fronting two recesses. The doors shown are light and easily hung. Chipboard may be used but is rather heavy and tends to be difficult to hinge. Sliding doors may be used; if so, the mitred hardwood sub-frame may be dispensed with. The hardwood trim is purely a decorative feature to contrast with the painted softwood frame.

Fig. 54. 'Gim-Fit' Units
These are a novelty, or gimmick, furniture idea. They may be built from oddments often displayed outside 'Handy-Man' shops. Extra shelves may be rested on the edges of the locator strips. If desired, shelf housings may be stopped both at back and front to allow units to be visually pleasing from both sides.

Fig. 55. A Small Television Chair
All chair work demands well fitting joints. The suggested chair is best

Fig. 53.
This is a simple way to fill in recesses at the side of the chimney breast. The main frame is of softwood, 125 mm × 28 mm and is painted. The sub-frame moulding is in hardwood, polished. Doors are hardboard face on a softwood core. Door lippings are of hardwood and are glued and pinned on after the doors have been trial fitted to opening.
The interior may be fitted to requirements using the system shown in Fig. 48.

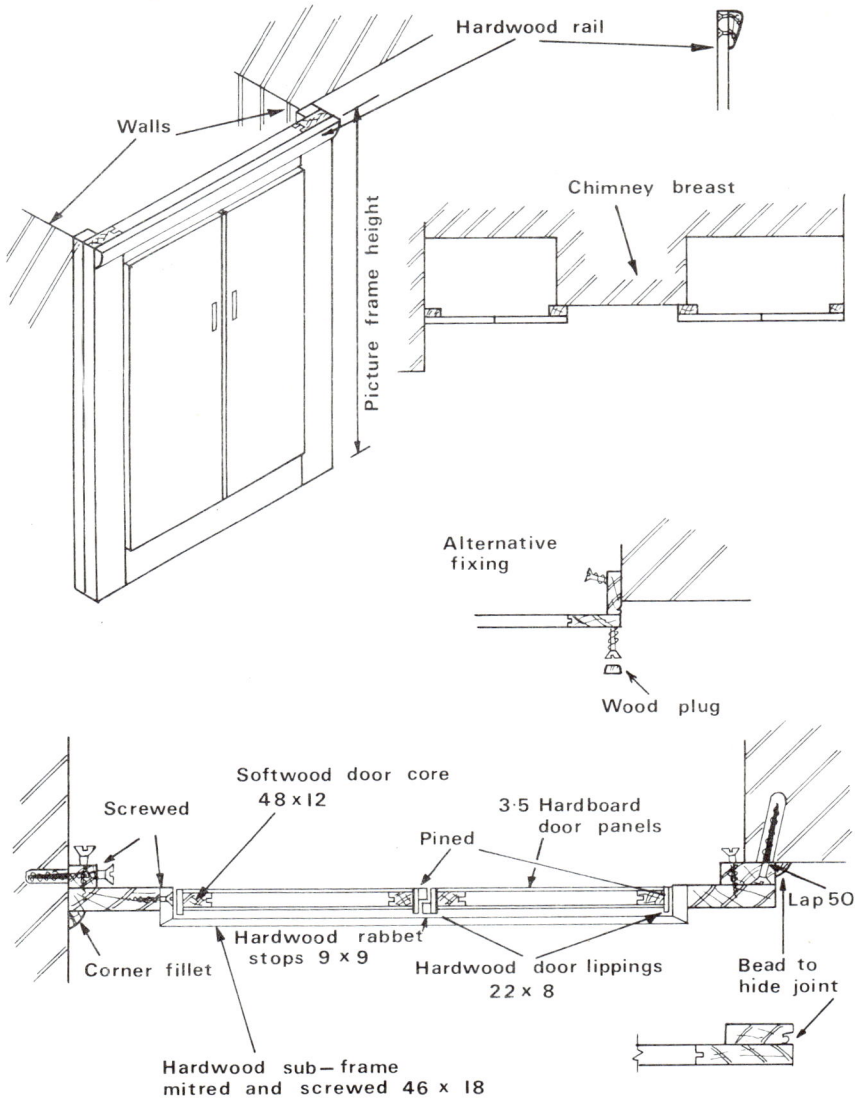

Hardwood rail

Walls

Picture frame height

Chimney breast

Alternative fixing

Wood plug

Screwed

Softwood door core
48 × 12

Pined

3·5 Hardboard door panels

Corner fillet

Hardwood rabbet stops 9 × 9

Hardwood door lippings
22 × 8

Lap 50

Bead to hide joint

Hardwood sub−frame mitred and screwed 46 × 18

Fig. 54.
This novelty furniture for the nursery may
be made up from plywood, blockboard or
chipboard offcuts, and may be veneered
or painted. 15 mm thick material is sufficient. The locators are of hardwood,
dyed and polished to bright colours.
All housing joints must be tightly fitted
and glued.

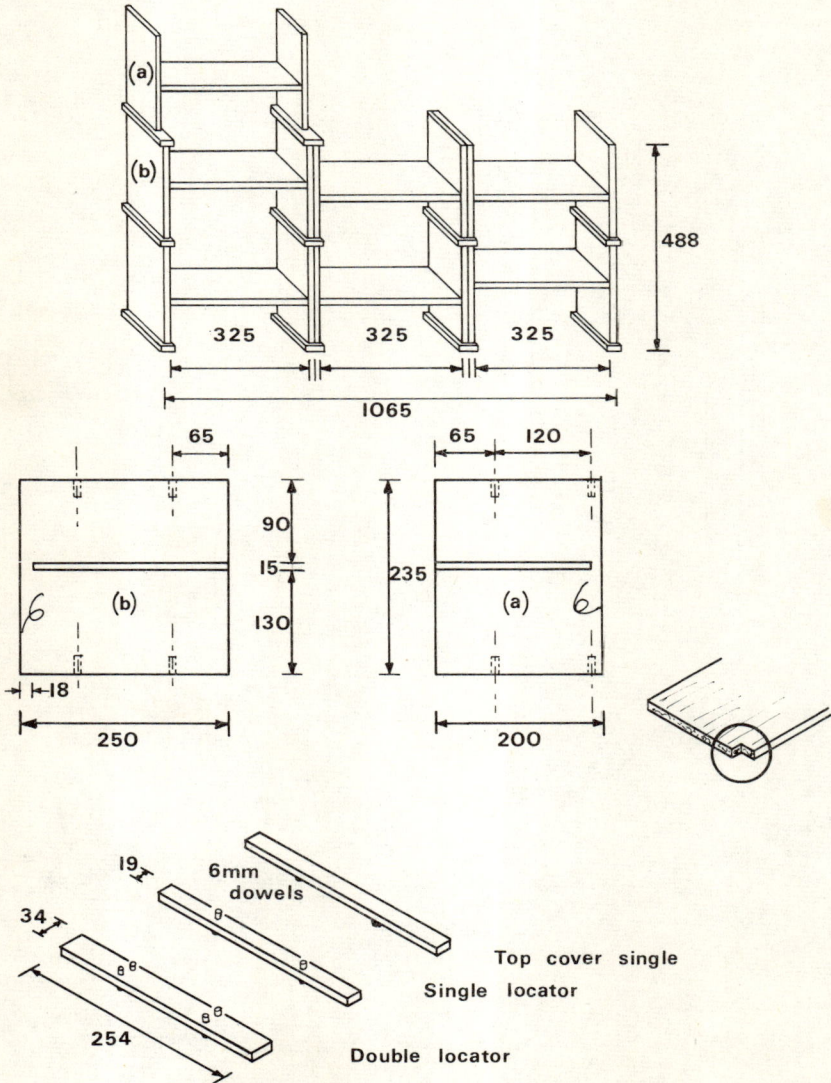

(a)

(b)

488

325   325   325

1065

65

90

15

130

(b)

250

18

235

65   120

(a)

200

19   6mm
         dowels

34

254

Top cover single

Single locator

Double locator

Fig. 55.

The fire-side chair shown has loose cushions with loose covers.

The legs are in clean softwood, as are the back frame and lower side rails.

The top side rails and the seat front rail are of 'Utile'.

Tenons are 9 mm; tight fitting and well glued.

Seat frame should be hardwood, preferably Beech.

Finish with clear Ronseal.

Seat angles

450 x 450 x 100
Block foam
with loose covers

Leg
Front rail

Staples Side rail

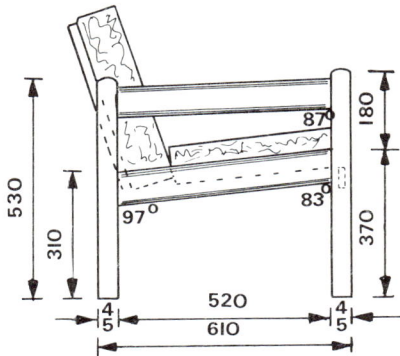

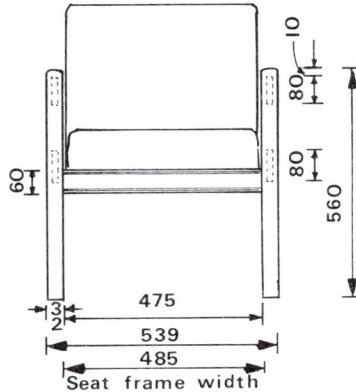

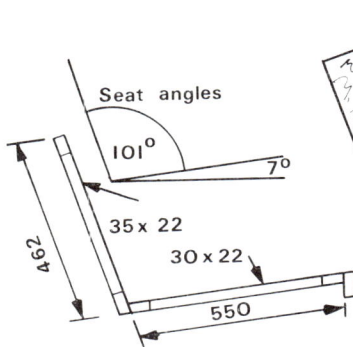

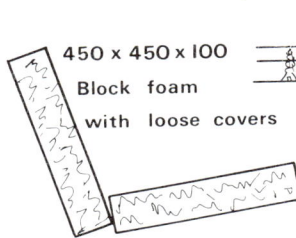

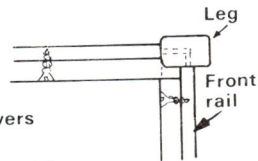

Springs 375 long before extension

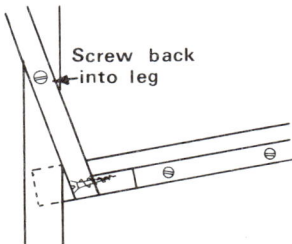

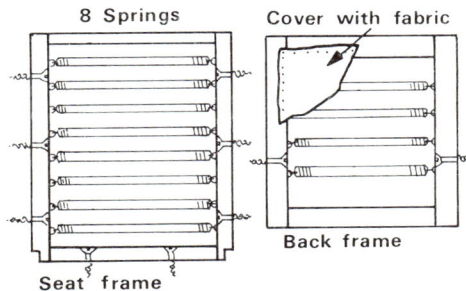

Screw back into leg

8 Springs

Cover with fabric

Seat frame

Back frame

made in two stages. The two side frames are made and assembled. From these check-measurements are made to ensure that the back and seat frames will fit. The joints between side rails and legs are made as deep as possible and only when these are firmly set are the two mortises for the front rail cut. This interlocks the two tenons.

The suggested combination of Utile and Deal is pleasing if used with a plain green covering fabric, but there is no reason why the chair should not be made from one timber all through, or other combinations tried. Spiral springs required about 10% extension, and this means that a spring bought at 450 mm must stretch across 495 mm.

Index

162